I, the Lord, Have Seen Thy Sorrow

An LDS Guide to Dealing with the Pain of Infidelity

Ruth Davidson

Gatehouse
MEDIA

Gatehouse Media
American Fork, UT 84003

I, the Lord, Have Seen Thy Sorrow
Copyright © 1999 Ruth Davidson. All rights reserved.

ISBN: 1-890828-18-1

HISTORY
3rd Edition: Summer 2010

PRINTED IN THE UNITED STATES OF AMERICA
10 9 8 7 6 5 4 3 2 1

"In all their afflictions he was afflicted. ...And in his love, and in his pity, he redeemed them, and bore them, and carried them."

—D&C 133:53

Contents

Foreword

"My husband is seeing another woman."

"When my friend Rebecca* (*names have been changed) first spoke these words to me, I wanted to stop time for a moment. I somehow wanted to spare my heart the pain and anguish I knew would come as the full impact of what she said came through to me. *How many times would I have to go through this?* I wondered. *How many times would I have to watch a family being torn apart by infidelity and witness the pain and devastation brought about by another's sin?* Now it was happening to someone I loved deeply, someone very close to me whose pain I felt almost as keenly as my own. I wasn't sure I could stand seeing this happen to her and her young family.

All through the day and into the night I struggled with feelings of helplessness and anger. I felt anger toward the one who had chosen to break sacred marriage covenants and who had allowed selfishness and a wandering eye to threaten the sanctity of his family and his relationship with his spouse. I could hardly believe that he had allowed Satan to tempt him in a way that could ultimately destroy sacred family ties. *If he wants the other woman,* I thought angrily, *then let him have her.*

As night deepened and my troubled feelings increased, however, the import of what was happening slowly descended upon my soul. As I agonized over the situation, it seemed that for a brief moment I could glimpse eternity stretched out before me. Not only did I see an entire family's welfare at stake, there was an eternal soul in jeopardy of losing everything of value to him.

I knew with this realization I couldn't sit idly by and watch. If there was anything I could do, I needed to help. I turned to the Lord in reaching, heartfelt prayer. My prayers continued on into the night and throughout the next day. "Please, Father," I pleaded. "Please help him. Please help him realize what he's doing and what's happening to his family. Help him to be able to see the eternal consequences of the choices he's making. Please help him stop sinning and turn his heart back toward his family, if at all possible.

"Please give Rebecca your help and sustenance as she deals with him for if anyone, she will be the key to his return. Be with her and strengthen her; stay beside her and comfort her. Help her to know she is loved when the closest person to her on earth has no love for her. Help her have the capacity to heal from all the pain and anguish she's experiencing.

"And if her husband chooses to leave her, please give Rebecca the capacity to carry on without him so she can be a support to her family. She will only be able to do this with your help.

"As for me, Father, help me know what I can do. It's not even happening to me yet I feel the pain and weight of it as if it were. If there's anything I can do, please help me understand what it is. Please bless me with the strength and comfort I need to be able to reach out and become a support to them at this time.

"Please let me help, Father. I want to help."

1

"I, the Lord, Have Seen the Sorrow" (Jacob 2:31)

When the Lord speaks of the numerous plagues which shall afflict the earth in the last days, I now include the plague of infidelity to one's spouse. This breaking of the sacred covenants of marriage brings some of the deepest heartache and greatest devastation to those involved. Spouses are affected; children, whether young or old, are affected; extended families, parents in particular, are affected; neighbors, friends and even business associates are affected.

Infidelity is not just a problem of the world. It seems to be growing in greater and greater proportion inside the Church of Jesus Christ of Latter-day Saints, as well. It is essential that as members of the Lord's Church we learn how to understand and effectively deal with the painful repercussions of this growing problem. We must learn to recognize and combat the intricate lies and deceptions used to justify infidelity.

"They're dropping like flies around me," one woman claimed in agonized amazement. Not only did she carry the burden of her own daughter's infidelity, four couples within her ward boundaries, one lifelong friend, a sister and also a cousin were involved in recent divorces brought about by the unfaithfulness of one of the spouses in the marriage relationship. She could scarcely handle the implications of it all.

As evil spreads its dark forces throughout the world, we will hear of more and more cases similar to this as Satan continues his unceasing war against families. More and more spouses will grapple with the devastation and heartache brought about by infidelity. Children, extended families, friends and acquaintances will feel the rippling effects of this great sin. Many will suffer greatly because of it.

This book speaks primarily to those whose hearts have been broken due to infidelity. There are many who are entering this uncharted territory without help, scarcely realizing what is happening in their lives. As there is a "pattern in all things" pertaining to righteousness, so are there patterns in all things pertaining to wickedness. (D&C 52:14) If those going through this can see and discern these patterns of wickedness, this can bring added strength to help them deal with the burdens they will be called upon to carry.

Those dealing with the pain of infidelity need to realize they are not alone in their sufferings. Not only have others gone through the devastation of such choices, there is One who has already felt their heartbreaks, borne their grief and sorrows, experienced their anguished emotions and carried their heavy burdens. He is anxiously awaiting the opportunity to carry those burdens again if they will only but turn to Him.

The Lord will shed tears with those who are hurting. He will encircle those who are vulnerable and broken within the arms of His healing love. He will not leave anyone comfortless. He will give anchors of promised eternal blessings to sustain those sons and daughters who are going through what will become some of the darkest days and the most turbulent times of their lives.

The only way to overcome the pain caused by infidelity is through the sustaining power of the Savior. This help from the Lord can be found from feasting daily upon the scriptures and from earnest, heartfelt prayer. It can be found in relinquishment—that is, "Not my will, but thine be done." (Luke 22:42) It can be found from the strength, healing power and protection of the priesthood and also from the comfort that can be found within the walls of the temple. The Lord's strength can thus become the strength of those who are struggling in faith to overcome the consequences of another's deep sins.

2

"This People Begin to Wax in Iniquity" *(Jacob 2:23)*

Rebecca, whose story began in the "Foreword" of this book, was not only devastated but shocked when she discovered that her husband had been seeing another woman. She had loved her husband deeply. She had been committed to her marriage and the sacred covenants made between them in the temple. She had every intention of working on the problems that had arisen between them.

What Rebecca didn't realize was that the conflict, contention and ongoing struggles that had arisen within her marriage could be attributed to her husband's continuing desires for another woman. Although "the spouse is the last to know," as seemed true in this case, there were other indications that her husband was "beginning to labor in sin." (Jacob 1:5) Every argument, disagreement or difference of opinion they had experienced since the first day of their marriage, some reaching even as far back as their engagement, had come to the forefront of their lives. She and her husband had begun arguing almost constantly, whenever there were chances for interaction.

Most of their disagreements, arguments she thought they had long since settled, seemed exacerbated and blown out of proportion. Usually the greatest proportion of the blame for these problems was thrust on her. Molehills had become mountains and nothing she said or did would resolve these issues to any degree.

Almost every encounter began to be filled with this type of contention. Her husband became easily offended at almost everything she said. He became angry, impatient and frustrated with not only her past mistakes but with her present behavior. He began criticizing everything she did. He criticized her cooking, the way she spent money, how she handled the children and the way the home was kept. He criticized her for her lack of understanding and compassion for him, for what he was going through and for what he wanted to do in his life. He claimed she did not understand him and that she never had— and possibly never would. He believed she either had too many problems of her own or had become too selfish and self-centered to look past herself and see his needs. *How could she claim she loved him,* he would ask her, *when it was obvious by the way she treated him that she never had? And if, as she insisted, she* did *love him, then why did he feel so misunderstood, unloved and unappreciated?*

Many of these heated arguments became the impetus behind him leaving the home and spending time elsewhere where he wouldn't have to deal with all the misery and heartache his wife continually caused him. As the contention increased over time, physical intimacy between them lessened and soon virtually disappeared. Rebecca contributed it to the disharmony between them.

Some of this contention tricked down to her husband's interaction with their children. He became frustrated with the noise of their playing, with their childish disagreements and with the usual demands of home life. The love he'd given and shown before had dissipated and he became sharp and impatient. The children reacted in various ways but their troubled behavior, agitation and withdrawal showed that they, too, had begun to sense that things were amiss at home. Most of them withdrew in different ways but each, without exception, showed evidence of the tension they felt in the home. For some it was a drastic drop in grades at school; others showed troubled behavioral patterns. The older children struggled to find their niches of security outside the home, spending more and more time with friends and less and less time at their place.

Signs of wear and neglect also began to appear both inside and outside the home as the family dealt with the deeper, more pressing issues that bombarded them. Cluttered messes, a dry and un-mowed lawn and beds of weeds were unusual for them but had become apparent. Chores her husband had usually completed were left undone.

The Contention

Despite all these signs, Rebecca still had no idea that her husband had begun seeing another woman, that this increase in contention and bickering had been indicative of the first stages of infidelity. She did not realize that the constant problems and incessant fighting had in essence become excuses—seemingly valid ones—for her husband to leave the home and go elsewhere to find solace.

When Rebecca did find out about third-party involvement, she became filled with both shock and bewilderment. Only in looking back did she recognize the circumstances in her family for what they had been. The contention had been indicative of a greater, carefully hidden problem. Knowingly or unknowingly, her husband had created from his behaviors the kind of situation that allowed him to rationalize his sinful actions as being justified.

In every situation where there is infidelity, there is similar behavior and similar contention. Growing, incessant contention and fighting, without being able to solve problems or come to any amicable solutions, is one of the first indications of something amiss and seems to come about as the straying partner seeks justification for sins already committed or for continuing desires for someone outside the marriage relationship. It is as if straying partners try to create the kinds of situations at home which allow them to feel justified in looking outward for support.

Straying partners have been taught the truth. They know the laws and commandments of God. They understand the Lord's directive to have one partner and one partner only, that the Lord places adultery and its attendant sins second only to murder. They know "the will of God concerning them, for it had been taught unto them." (3 Nephi 6:18) Only by rationalizing behavior in this manner—by creating the contention inside homes and with spouses that make straying partners believe they are justified in pursuing their outside relationships—can they live with themselves and the knowledge of what they're doing. Stephen R. Covey describes it this way:

> When we hear the first whispering of conscience, we do one of two things—we either act in harmony with it, or we immediately begin to rationalize—tell ourselves "rational lies"—as to why we should make some other choice. If we choose the first option, we feel peaceful.
> ...If we choose the second option, we feel disharmony and tension. We begin to justify our decision, often on the basis of external factors such as other people or circumstance. We typically begin blaming and accusing others. ...*We're each acting in ways that invoke in others the very negative behavior that becomes the excuse for our own.* (*First Things First*, p. 175, italics added)

The Lies

"There never was an adulterer," Bruce R. McConkie stated in *Mormon Doctrine*, "who was not also a liar; the two always go together. (p. 24) This statement speaks for itself. Whenever someone is being unfaithful, lies will always accompany the sin—lies about the past and present, lies about what is being done, lies about who someone is with, lies about what's happening at work, lies about what's happening to take that person away from the family and so on. Many become so embedded in these lies that they soon cannot differentiate truth from error.

Some become so well-versed in lies and deception that the spouses have no idea their straying partners are leading double lives. For example, one woman who had been married and was having an affair claimed that the lack of physical intimacy between her husband and her stemmed from a supposed sexual assault she'd had after being repeatedly stalked. As she pretended to go to counseling, to the authorities and to other places where she claimed she was "dealing with her problem," she used this time to see the man with whom she was having an affair. She told this same story of sexual assault to extended family and friends. Because no one knew of the affair, no one had reason to doubt her. Many expressed sympathy and concern; prayers were even offered in her behalf.

It wasn't until after the affair was discovered that her husband began to suspect that her story might not be true. As he began to check out the facts related to her story, he discovered that no report on the supposed attack and stalking had ever been filed. The authorities did not know of the attack, as she'd claimed. This story, in essence, became the lie she used to try to cover her tracks as she spent time with another man.

The lies come in different ways but lies will always be there. Until a thorough repentance is made, those lies continue. It becomes easy for a committed spouse, even if he or she wants to try to rebuild the relationship, to distrust everything a straying partner says or does. Lying has become an integral part of that person's nature and it takes time and prolonged effort to change.

3

"Ye Have Broken the Hearts" (Jacob 2:35)

To watch Rebecca deal with the sorrow and pain that came as she discovered the truth about her husband seeing another woman was a heart-wrenching experience. It seemed that nothing could hurt her more deeply than his betrayal of what she thought they had shared, worked for and built between them. His emotional abandonment of her—the complete loss of concern, love and caring he'd once had for her—gave rise to an anguished loneliness she'd never experienced in her life.

Before she went through this sorrow after finding out the truth, however, she had experienced other emotional trauma of which she was only beginning to become aware. Her husband's previous contentious behavior toward her had wounded her deeply. She had been greatly affected by the emotional attacks that had come from him during times of fighting and bickering. The hostility and animosity he'd shown had taken a heavy emotional toll.

For many, the repercussions of the contention created by an unfaithful spouse can leave devastating emotional scars. This devastation has a specific basis. As straying spouses become victims to Satan's enticements and his deceit, the adversary can easily prod them into attacking, belittling, criticizing or undermining their partners in attempts to wound, hurt or destroy them. Wittingly or unwittingly, straying spouses become tools of destruction to those they once loved.

Satan knows our weaknesses and insecurities. He sees what causes us self-doubt and fear. He understands what hurts us or causes us worry. He knows what can make us feel inadequate or unworthy. He can easily use someone in his grasp, who is already buying into his lies and deception, to use this knowledge to inflict pain or injury in a partner.

Straying spouses often create vulnerabilities in their partners where none have existed before or work on current vulnerabilities, such as lack of self-confidence or low self-esteem, to an even greater extent. Personality traits a spouse might struggle with may be belittled. Current or past behaviors may be attacked as "destructive," "selfish," "self-righteous" or "manipulative." A spouse may be turned on as "evil" or "unrighteous." Physical appearance or dressing standards may also be criticized.

Unfaithful partners many times claim their spouses are mentally unstable, that they are not capable of maintaining healthy, viable relationships because they are not whole or that they will never be able to become whole with who or what they are, with their chosen thought patterns or because of what they've gone through in the past. Straying partners often claim their spouses are immature, incapable of making any changes necessary for healthy relationships and therefore it is useless to try to work with them.

Attacks like these come when, as mentioned previously, spouses begin to rationalize behaviors or sins that cannot in good conscience be justified. Many times a committed spouse is open to these attacks, especially when he or she is most vulnerable—when that person is unaware of the unholy choices a partner is making or when he or she is first dealing with the painful discovery of a spouse's unfaithfulness.

The committed spouse, who still often feels great love, caring and compassion for a partner, is almost always open to these attacks. The trust that had supposedly been built over time has not yet been questioned and therefore many have not shielded their hearts from the destructive behaviors going on. Because they are open to these attacks, many become deeply wounded. As the prophet Jacob put it in the *Book of Mormon,* "Many hearts died, pierced with deep wounds." (Jacob 2:35)

For one woman, the contention and criticism from her husband during his undiscovered affair gave rise to a whole host of problems from her past she had supposed she had worked through. As she struggled to address the issues that resurfaced in her life, she worked on them amidst the constant hostility and criticism from her husband. As the tension in her home and marriage arose, she became troubled and agitated. She became full of self-doubt and battled feelings of unworthiness and lack of self-esteem. She could scarcely eat or sleep. She slowly became depressed and began losing the ability to cope with even simple tasks that she'd never struggled with before, tasks such as housekeeping and getting ready for the day. Sleeping longer hours soon became her only escape from the problems plaguing her. Whereas she'd loved getting out and socializing before, she withdrew from social activity and situations where she'd have to interact.

Because of this pattern of behavior, this woman reached a point of crisis where she almost suffered a nervous breakdown. As she neared this point, she began seeking professional help. Not long afterward, she learned the truth about her husband's affair. After the affair had been discovered, she could begin to see how her husband's infidelity and the contention in their marriage had given rise to the current problems she had been experiencing. She could finally see the situation for what it was. With help from her family and continued help from trained professionals, her stability and mental health returned. Once she knew the root of her problems, she could move forward and deal with the situation for what it was without carrying the burden of the blame she'd previously placed upon herself.

Another woman handled the contention from her husband differently. As accusation upon accusation came from him—"You don't love me as you should; you don't do this or that for me; you're never here for me, like you're supposed to be; you only think of yourself and your needs, never what's important to me; you don't understand me"—she would accept the blame for everything happening in their marriage and agree to change, as he "needed her to do if their marriage was going to work." She took upon herself the weight of his unhappiness and promised to become what her husband claimed she should be. As time passed and she truly tried to make the changes he demanded, she told him in exasperation one day, "I've tried everything you've asked me to do and it still doesn't make you happy. *You* are the one that is going to have to make *yourself* happy." Not longer after this, this woman discovered that her husband had been having an affair. Discovering the truth, despite how painful it was, made it easier for her to deal with the realities of her situation and move forward with her life.

This is true for many individuals dealing with infidelity in their relationships. Understanding a straying partner's behavior and the contention that has arisen between them for what it is becomes an essential part of the healing process. A spouse who has remained committed to the relationship does not need to carry the burden that it was his or her current or past behavior that drove another spouse away. He or she can accept the peace of knowing that the contention is a *fruit of* rather than the *cause of* a spouse's infidelity.

4

"They Seek to Excuse Themselves in Committing Whoredoms" *(Jacob 2:23)*

Once Rebecca became aware of her husband's infidelity, he could no longer continue his double life of deception and betrayal without her awareness of what was going on. Because of this, their marriage reached a point of crisis. Her husband had to make a choice. He could either continue his relationship with this other woman and lose his wife and family or stop the outside relationship and attempt to rebuild his marriage.

As he struggled with this decision, Rebecca faced her own set of choices. Even if her husband did decide to return and attempt to salvage their marriage, was she willing to accept him back? Could she live with his betrayal and try to work on a marriage that had become filled with contention and dishonesty? Would it be best to leave the kind of relationship they had now, a relationship that made both her and her children feel uprooted and insecure, and take her children elsewhere where they might heal and go on?

Although Rebecca strongly considered divorce due to her concerns, her intense pain and hurt—and because of the continuing contention in their relationship—she felt directed by the Spirit to stay within her marriage and attempt to begin the process of healing with her husband, who did choose to stay with her.

For many, continuing a marital relationship after discovering a spouse's unfaithfulness is not an option. Although that person may feel a willingness to try to forgive and move toward healing, a straying spouse may not choose to stay and give the marriage a second chance. Often a straying spouse's desire for another person has become so great the straying spouse is willing to give up everything eternal for this other relationship.

If the straying spouse does choose to leave a partner, rarely can that decision be swayed. Often nothing can make a difference in the thinking and thought patterns adopted to justify sinful behaviors. No warnings from priesthood leaders will have any influence if the choice has already been made. No show of love, no gifts or charitable acts of service on the part of the committed spouse will change a partner's mind. Marriage counseling will not make a difference at this point.

One woman spoke of her husband choosing to leave her despite her desires to try to rebuild their relationship. "The Lord had to teach me," she said, "that no matter what amount of love I had to offer my husband, he still had the choice to turn away from me. I learned that the Lord had given us all the gift of free agency and I could not take that away from him."

Another woman spoke of a similar experience, expressing the idea that even if she had been a perfect spouse in the past, her husband still would have found reasons to leave her. This lesson was impressed upon her mind one day. She had been thinking over the past, depressed that her husband had chosen to end their marriage and leave her for another woman. She knew her imperfections and weaknesses and agonized over how these must have attributed to her husband's behavior and his desires for someone else. She began thinking of things she might have done to stop his infidelity.

Perhaps should could have understood him better, listened more, fixed better meals. Perhaps she could have been better aware of the times of stress that had made him vulnerable to outside enticements. Perhaps if she had met his emotional and physical needs, nothing would have happened. Perhaps if she'd had a "more lovely character" then he might not have strayed. As she continued to dwell on these thoughts, she happened to look at a picture of the Savior hanging on the wall above her. "He was perfect," came the impression into her mind, "and had the most lovely character of anyone on earth. Yet others turned from Him."

She quickly understood the lesson being taught. Christ had been perfect in His love, in His example and in His offerings of service and yet others still turned from him in hatred and anger. This woman came to understand that there came a point that no matter what she'd done or what she hadn't done, what she had said or how she had acted, she could not have swayed her husband's choice to leave. He had chosen his path and none of her actions would have made a difference.

The Lines, the Excuses

For every straying spouse who chooses to leave an eternal mate, that person must "still a conscience." In other words, that person must buy into a selected thought pattern of rationalization in order to justify sinful behaviors. New realities are created in their minds and they become blind to truth and fact. The excuses vary but they form a specific pattern: *"Because you did this or because you didn't do this, or because you are this way or because you aren't this way, I am justified in the decisions I'm making."* These arguments are most often filled with irony, hypocrisy, justification and untruth. Many are so filled with subtle and intricate arguments they can lead the mind into a maze of confusion. Examples of some arguments, taken from different experiences, are as follows:

•*"A third party has nothing to do with the problems in our marriage. These problems have been with us and between us ever since we've known each other. Don't try to blame this on an outside party when the fault lies with you and me, not with anyone else."*

•*"I've lived with you and your problems for years and it's now time that I begin to look out for myself. I deserve to find happiness. And if this long-awaited happiness comes from being with _____, then so be it. I owe it to myself to be happy."*

•*"For years I've denied truth and righteousness by staying in a relationship that is destroying me. The Lord knows if I stay with you and am influenced by your thinking and behaviors, I will be destroyed. He's guiding me this way. I've never felt greater spiritual wholeness or happiness than I do now. How can this be wrong? His truth has set me free. The Lord is showing me the road to wholeness and it will not be with you. It will be with someone else."*

•*"This person treats me so much better (with compassion, love, understanding and caring) than you ever did, you who claim to love me. I want to be treated this way. I deserve to be treated this way."*

•*"I never really loved you. I only married you because…"*

•*"Maybe we have made a mistake in committing adultery, but we can move forward and the Lord will forgive us. The Lord is all-knowing and compassionate. His atonement will help us become clean again. It is you who carries the greater sin. You're being self-righteous and hypocritical. You blame us and don't forgive us. You're the one with the real problem. The atonement can apply to us because we are trying to do what's right. It will not apply to you because you're so full of self-righteousness and hypocrisy."*

•*"If it hadn't been _____ who came into my life, I would have had an affair with someone else. It was waiting to happen because I've been so unhappy and dissatisfied in our marriage. You have never met my needs and you never will. I had to find someone who would."*

•*"Even if things don't work out between me and _____, I would never get back with you because I could never be happy with you. Continuing our marriage is not an option for me. I won't return to a relationship where I've had so much pain and misunderstanding."*

•*"My patriarchal blessing describes my spouse as being a certain way and you are not that way. You don't live up to those promises. I obviously made the wrong choice and I need to leave."*

The foregoing true examples are a sample of some of the rationalizations that have been used to justify sinful behavior. Always these excuses are there, in varying forms, whenever anyone has been unfaithful. However, as Alma said to his son Corianton, "Do not endeavor to excuse yourself *in the least point* because of your sins." (Alma 42:30, italics added) The Lord also warns, "Cursed are all those that lift up the heel against mine anointed and cry they have sinned when they have not sinned before me. ...Those who cry transgression do it because they are the servants of sin, *and are the children of disobedience themselves.*" (D&C 121:16-17, italics added)

When Others Don't See the Truth

Some of the most painful hurt that can accompany rationalizations comes when others on the outside of a relationship, who don't know the situation for what it is, adopt the thinking of the unfaithful partner. Friends, family members and even children of those marriages often buy into these thought patterns. For example, one elderly couple strictly forbade their son-in-law to "ever step foot in our house again, not after all the pain and anguish you've caused our daughter." They believed the lies she told about him to justify her adulterous relationship. Not only did this man have to deal with the hostility of his wife and losing her to infidelity, he had to deal with the alienation and animosity of her extended family. It became an extremely painful and lonely time for him.

Another young bishop, after hearing the complaints of a husband he had been counseling (who happened to be in the beginning stages of an adulterous relationship), told this man's wife, "If you don't start doing some of these things and working on these negative behaviors you have, you're going to be losing your husband. You need to change." Not until a seasoned stake president, who had dealt with many affairs during his tenure, talked to this young bishop did that bishop see the marriage problems for what they were. His reactions, however, added to this woman's feelings of pain and devastation.

One woman found comfort for dealing with this type of rationalization in a priesthood blessing she received. "There is no room for infidelity," she was told. "The way is simple and clear and few there be that find it." This knowledge helped her. She came to understand that no matter how intricate or subtle the arguments, no matter how varied or seemingly valid were the excuses, the Lord accepted none of them. As the Lord states, He "cannot walk in crooked paths, neither doth he vary from that which he hath said; neither hath he a shadow of turning from the right to the left, or from that which is right to that which is wrong." (Alma 7:20) The way is simple and clear and few there be that find it: *There is no excuse for infidelity!*

24

More Hardened in Iniquity

Until the repentance process begins, transgressors who choose to buy into Satan's lies and deceptions justifying infidelity will become more hardened in iniquity—that is, they will sink deeper and deeper into sin and the false realities they've created. Lies and rationalization continue and become truth to them as they refuse to change thinking or listen to anyone else's views on the situation.

Many times sinning parties have been able to rationalize their sins to the point where they feel perfectly justified in continuing regular church activity and feel worthy to do so. One woman still felt she could attend the temple with her husband as she carried another man's baby, a baby her husband thought was his. Her partner, who had engaged in three known affairs, continued temple attendance as well.

Oftentimes, as straying spouses begin a downward spiral, they "wax more gross in their iniquities." (Alma 8:28) Some lose their testimonies, their faith in God and contact with the church. Church inactivity may be justified on the basis that church members are hypocritical, full of self-righteousness and the lack of Christ-like love. *Why should they go anywhere where they are not accepted, especially to a place where all these people are claiming they're trying to become like the Savior and are so far from it?* they might ask.

Many times when transgressors become hardened in sin, it is only through outside events of hardship that the Lord can begin to humble them. Often the Lord must bring them to their knees in humility before He can begin to work with them and start the process necessary for them to repent, return to Him and become clean again. The Lord has said, "I will not succor my people in the day of their transgressions; but I will hedge up their ways that they prosper not; and their doings shall be as a stumbling block before them." He continues, "If my people shall show filthiness, they shall reap the east wind, which bringeth immediate destruction." (Mosiah 7:29-31) The Lord has also warned, "Inasmuch as you are found transgressors you cannot escape my wrath in your lives." (D&C 104:8)

"I am angry with this people," He has stated, "and my fierce anger is kindled against them; for their hearts have waxed hard, and their ears are dull of hearing, and their eyes cannot see afar off. ...[They have] gone astray, and have denied me, and have sought their own counsels in the dark." (Moses 6:27-28)

Because of this, the Lord claims, "I will return their iniquities upon their own heads." (3 Nephi 20:28) The Lord chastens those who have sinned that they might repent and return to Him. "Verily, thus saith the Lord unto you whom I love, and whom I love I also chasten that their sins may be forgiven, for with the chastisement I prepare a way for their deliverance in all things out of temptation, and I have loved you." (D&C 95:1)

This chastening comes in various ways. For example, many times the Lord uses financial difficulties to soften hearts. "Their basket shall not be full, their houses and their barns shall perish," He tells us. (D&C 121:20) Sometimes hardships and difficulties arise in jobs or careers. Outside associations or other relationships may become strained and contentious. Truly, their own doings become a "stumbling block" before those who sin. (Mosiah 7:29)

Irony lies in the fact that many times the adulterous relationship a spouse has been willing to give up all things eternal for will in the end become the "stumbling block" the Lord describes. When relationships are built upon selfishness and lust, they do not last. Unless true repentance comes about, "they themselves shall be despised by those that flattered them." (D&C 121:20) The happiness they supposed they found between

26

them disintegrates into a smoldering heap of ashes. For example, one woman who was having an affair with a married man exclaimed loudly to this man's wife, "I love your husband!" They were soon after married. Several years later, after this relationship and marriage ended, this woman was heard to say of this man, "He is the most selfish person I've ever met in my life."

Many times what is seen on the outside of an adulterous relationship is not indicative of what is happening on the inside. For example, a couple in a ward, whose marriage began after an adulterous relationship, seemed happy and content. Every time they were together, they laughed, held hands, smiled and acted as if everything in their lives remained happy and peaceful. "It's odd to me," one of their neighbors told her husband, "how they can be so happy after what happened."

"You have no idea," the husband countered. He had been talking to the husband in that marriage who had shared with him some of the hardships and problems they were having together and between the two families they were trying to combine. They were struggling and having a difficult time. It was not easy and all was not well. Their superficial happiness was not indicative of what was happening inside their home or hearts.

The only way to return to true happiness is clear. Those who have sinned must "turn to the Lord with full purpose of heart, and put [their] trust in him, and serve him with all diligence of mind." Then the Lord will, "according to his own will and pleasure, deliver [them] out of bondage." (Mosiah 7:33)

Accepting any type of rationalization for infidelity or participating in an adulterous relationship is bondage. Satan has literally grasped those who have done so with his chains and has encircled them with his demons. Although they have "joy in their works for a season, …by and by the end cometh. (3 Nephi 27:11) Happiness will not be found in iniquity. It never has been and never will be. (Alma 41:10) It is contrary to the nature of happiness. Only by turning to the Lord, by truly repenting and seeking forgiveness can true happiness be found.

Hope for Those Bound by Iniquity

I find comfort in the fact that one of Alma's sons, Corianton, who "forsook the ministry" and "did go over into the land of Siron…after the harlot Isabel," (Alma 39:3) returned to the ministry with his father and brothers. He was later called a man of God "like unto Ammon, the son of Mosiah, yea, and also the other sons of Mosiah." (Alma 48:18) Although, as his father had claimed, "Whosoever murdereth against the light and knowledge of God, it is not easy for him to obtain forgiveness," (Alma 39:6) Corianton had obviously heeded his father's counsel and begun the long road toward repentance.

There have been families healed—Rebecca's, for one—because of a straying spouse's willingness to give up darkness and turn once again toward the light. Another woman humbled herself deeply to forgive her husband who had fathered another child and then accepted him back into her home so they could begin to forgive, heal and move on. Another man, although he lost his wife and family due to his infidelity, became re-baptized and centered his life once again on the Savior. The atonement is real. It does work for those who have sinned. The key is repentance. The return to wholeness comes through our Lord and Savior, Jesus Christ. He will not give up on any who have strayed but His "hand is stretched out still." (2 Nephi 15:25) He waits unendingly for those who have strayed to return to Him.

When True Repentance Starts

When a sinning soul begins the process of true repentance, not only will that person acknowledge faults and wrongs done but, as Spencer W. Kimball set forth, that person "convinced of his sin and suffering godly sorrow for it in humility is reduced—or rather in this case elevated—to tears. Thus he expresses anguish for his folly and for the grief it has brought to the innocent." (*Miracle of Forgiveness*, p. 60)

Many will be able to discern when true repentance like this starts. One woman, Jenny, waited for years to see true repentance in the life of a family member who had participated in adultery. That family member claimed to be repentant but Jenny saw no indication of it. *Perhaps I won't witness the process,* Jenny thought. *Perhaps it's such a quiet, inward thing that I won't see it happening.*

During this time, however, Jenny felt prompted to visit a friend she hadn't seen in years. This friend had been brought up in the Church but had gone on in sin and rebellion, making many unrighteous choices along the way. When they visited, Jenny became surprised to find her friend going through a horrendous time, being barely able to sleep or function. Her friend was suffering with depression and felt plagued by extreme anxiety. She had become overwhelmed with everyday life and felt hopeless and lost. The depths of her despair were powerful and at the same time inescapable. The sorrow and anguish seemed to encompass her entire being. This sorrow seemed similar to Alma's when he stated, "My soul was harrowed up to the greatest degree and racked with all my sins. Yea, I did remember all my sins and iniquities, for which I was tormented with the pains of hell." (Alma 36:12-13) Her sorrow seemed similar to Zeezrom's which "did harrow up his mind

29

until it did become exceedingly sore, having no deliverance." (Alma 15:3)

"This is what you will see," the Spirit whispered to Jenny. "This is how you will know when true sorrowing unto repentance begins." Jenny then knew what to watch for, that this type of sorrowing would precede the repentance process she wanted to see in her family member's life. She knew she hadn't seen it yet but felt assured that she would. She further believed this kind of deep sorrowing would ultimately lead the one she loved toward true repentance, the confessing and complete forsaking of sin. (D&C 58:43)

5

Battle Over the Souls

For those who have witnessed the process of infidelity, the scenario might have gone something like this: *A husband or wife is nothing more than a friend of another person—a person at work, a neighbor, a partner of one of the couples they see together or an acquaintance. Although the two of them start spending time together, it doesn't mean anything. They just enjoy being together and speaking occasionally. What they're doing is completely innocent and involves no wrongdoing.*

Soon their "sharing" moves toward something deeper where both parties begin seeking understanding and emotional support from each other. They begin talking frequently. They discuss everyday concerns and daily happenings with work or their families. They discuss what they want to do with their lives—their dreams, goals and ambitions. Their relationship feels free, simple and exciting, unfettered by the problems and stresses of their current lives.

They begin to feel happy being understood and listened to by this person who is paying so much attention to them. They feel excited to be treated kindly, to be cared for and noticed like this. Soon they begin discussing all of their problems they have at home, problems they've had or are having with their current spouses.

Suddenly their current spouses don't seem as wonderful as this person who is willing to share with them. Their spouses don't listen as well as this other person listens. Their spouses don't offer the same understanding, support or concern that this other person offers.

"Come to think of it, why not?" they ask themselves. "Didn't our current spouses promise they'd do all these things when we married? Didn't they promise to love us and care for us? Didn't they promise to help us and support us? Then why don't they? Why don't we feel the same sort of happiness with them as we do when we're together?"

"It must be because our current spouses are not very good partners," they answer. "They're selfish and self-centered and in many ways dysfunctional. They are not capable of maintaining loving relationships. In fact, as we look back on our marriages, we can see hundreds of examples of times when our spouses were doing all these destructive behaviors.

"Remember this? Remember that? Oh, I'd forgotten about that, but I can see how it is indicative of all the problems my spouse has. My spouse is truly unhealthy, full of sin and hypocrisy. My spouse is not capable of a healthy relationship.

"No wonder we're not happy in our marriages," they conclude. "We've never really been happy. We couldn't have made our marriages work no matter how hard we tried because our spouses are not capable of loving or understanding us. No wonder we find so much wholeness and happiness when we're together. We share true love. We share true caring. It's strange but this is the first time we've ever felt complete."

These straying spouses then decide, "We have reason to be angry with our partners. The animosity and anger we feel towards them comes from years of pent-up frustration. It's time we assert ourselves. It's time we finally look out for Number One and not put ourselves second like we have for so many years. It's time we make the choices that help us become happy.

"In order to do so, we must show our spouses how imperfect and unhealthy they are. We must show them how selfish and shortsighted they've become. We need to make them see how all of their actions have been self-centered and selfish."

The spouses begin fighting back.

"See?" their partners say. "See how contentious, unhappy, angry and dysfunctional these people are? See how unloving, unkind and selfish they've become? See how rotten our marriages are and how rotten our spouses have become? They treat us horribly.

"It feels good to see the truth and finally be free. We're so lucky to have each other. We can give each other everything we've always wanted—love, understanding, compassion and concern."

Individually they conclude, "I've finally found the happiness I've always yearned for and it's with you. I'm going to do everything I need to do to spend my life and time with you. I deserve to be with you. You're the one who makes me happy."

These types of thoughts and thought patterns run as a common thread throughout almost all cases of infidelity. During this process, physical intimacy may or may not be a part of what happens. This does not make a difference. The cycle is the same; the results are the same. The Lord warns us not only about adultery but about adultery of the heart. "Whosoever looketh on a woman, to lust after her, hath committed adultery already in his heart," He has told us. (3 Nephi 12:28) He has also said, "He that looketh upon a woman to lust after her shall deny the faith, and shall not have the Spirit; and if he repents not he shall be cast out." (D&C 42:23)

Some feel that if they haven't participated in the actual act of adultery with the person they're seeing that everything is fine and that everything they've done can be justified. This is simply not the case. As Spencer W. Kimball said, "There are those married people who permit their eyes to wander and their hearts to become vagrant, who think it is not improper to flirt a little, to share their hearts and have desire for someone other than the wife or the husband. The Lord says in definite terms, 'Thou shalt love thy wife with all thy heart, and shalt cleave to her and none else.'" (*Miracle of Forgiveness*, p. 250) This not only includes physical but emotional fidelity.

Outside Intervention

Those on the outside of a relationship who care deeply about those involved in sin may try to step in to warn transgressors about their choices. Some of the reactions they might hear are similar to the following:

•*"You don't know the real story of what happened in my marriage. You've only heard my spouse's side of the story. If you had walked in my shoes and had gone through all I've gone through, you would know how truly awful it's been. You would understand why I'm making these choices."*

•*"Many couples are separated; many get divorced. You just need to accept it and deal with it. Handle it. It's my problem. I'm the one being affected. Let me worry about the consequences. This isn't your concern."*

•*"Everything will work out. The Lord knows the end from the beginning. He knew I would make these choices and He knew this would happen. He loves me. He will work with me and help me repent. That's what His atonement is for. I was included in that. I'm trying to repent. But repentance does not mean getting back with my spouse. I would never do that. I could never be happy or fulfilled if I did."*

• *"There's no way you could understand how terrible my marriage has been unless you lived with my spouse. If you had, you would understand my pain and the reasons I need to leave this awful relationship. You wouldn't be so critical of my decisions. You are critical because you haven't gone through what I have. You're being self-righteous and judgmental."*

• *"If you're worried about my choices because you think that I'm going to turn my back on my spouse or my children, you shouldn't be. Haven't I always taken care of them? I will continue to take care of them even if I'm not in the house. Don't concern yourself about that."*

• *"I've put myself aside for so many years to stay in this relationship. I can no longer do that. It will destroy me as a person. Besides, I need to finally put myself first and watch out for my emotional and spiritual needs. The only way I can do that is by leaving my marriage and continuing on in the paths I've chosen. I want to be happy and I owe it to myself to be happy. Nothing will stop me from doing what I know is right."*

• *"I've felt closer to the Lord more than I ever have as I've made these decisions. I keep getting answers from Him daily. I've never felt more peace or more self-assurance about anything I've done before. I know this is right. Nothing you can do or say will change my mind, not when I know the Lord is guiding my paths like He is."*

Sometimes transgressors ask, as the wicked Amalekite angrily asked Aaron in the *Book of Mormon*, "How knowest thou the thought and intent of our hearts? How knowest thou that we have cause to repent? How knowest thou that we are not a righteous people?" (Alma 21:6) In other words they're asking, "What right do you have to judge me? You don't know my heart or what I've gone through. You have no right to sit in

35

judgment on me or what I'm doing when you don't really know me or what's going on in my life. Stay out of this."

As these types of rationalizations and justifications become deep-set and rigid, many on the outside feel helpless in knowing what to do. Perhaps they tried to help but received reactions of anger or hostility from those who are sinning. Offense might have been taken where no offense was intended, only expressions of concern regarding the road being taken. Sometimes friendship or influence is sacrificed in an effort to help another see destructive behaviors and decisions.

Those hearing rationalizations and excuses often want to ask, as Amulek did, "Why hath Satan got so great hold upon your hearts? Why will ye yield yourselves unto him that he may have power over you, to blind your eyes, that ye will not understand the words which are spoken, according to their truth?" (Alma 10:25) They might wonder, as Nephi did, "How could you have given way to the enticing of him who is seeking to hurl away your souls down to everlasting misery and endless wo?" (Helaman 7:16)

Some who have experienced reactions of alienation and anger from sinning parties may feel there is nothing they can do to make a difference in their lives. They might wish to wash their hands of the situation and move on, accepting defeat. Satan would have us feel this way. He would have us stop our faith and prayers in behalf of those making these grave eternal choices. He wants us to give up on them because then he can move forward, undeterred, with the destruction he's already begun.

The Lord commands His children that "they should gather themselves together oft, and join in fasting and mighty prayer in behalf of the welfare of the souls of those who [know] not God." (Alma 6:6) We must continue to do this for those involved in sin if they are ever to receive help. One woman who had begun to sorrow and feel the loss of a close family member to infidelity was ready to give up her faith and prayers on that family member's behalf. She felt discouraged and defeated. The adulterous relationship the family member had participated in was moving toward a marriage and there was nothing she could do or say to stop it. In a priesthood blessing given to help her, she was told in essence, "Your faith is still a compelling force in the lives of those for whom you are concerned. The Lord cannot bless others unless they have faith. Therefore, the Lord appreciates your faith in their behalf. Our vision is short. We cannot always see the Lord's plan. Through prayer and through faith, the Lord's Spirit can be more near them."

This woman then knew that the Lord still needed her faith and prayers in order to work His hand in the lives of those for whom she had been concerned. She knew that "if there be no faith among the children of men God can do no miracle among them." (Ether 12:12) She continued her faith and prayers until the Lord told her in a subsequent blessing to "leave them in His hands." She then knew her faith and prayers had been sufficient for Him to work His will and that she could now, as Mosiah did with his son Ammon, "trust [them] unto the Lord." (Alma 19:23)

In the battle against infidelity, a battle which must be very similar to the battles we fought in the war in heaven, we will not be alone. The Lord will send His Spirit to teach and enlighten those trying to do His will. Through scriptures, through impressions and through priesthood blessings, He will give inspiration regarding ways to proceed forward. He knows how to direct us in handling all things pertaining to wickedness. We must trust that He "knoweth the weakness of man and how to succor them who are tempted." (D&C 62:1)

37

For one woman, the Lord compared in her mind the straying party she was dealing with to the Lord's dealings with Zion. She found insights in the scriptures to strengthen, help, comfort and direct her. "They were found transgressors," she read, "therefore they must needs be chastened." (D&C 101:41) "I, the Lord, will contend with Zion, and chasten her until she overcomes and is clean before me," she also read. (D&C 90:36) "This is a blessing which I have promised after your tribulations, and the tribulations of your brethren—your redemption, and the redemption of your brethren." (D&C 103:13)

The Spirit enlightened her mind as she read these scriptures. She came to understand that the straying party she had prayed for, after going through tribulation and the chastening hand of the Lord, would ultimately return through His power. She knew that "after their temptations, and much tribulation, behold, I, the Lord, will feel after them, and if they harden not their hearts, and stiffen not their necks against me, they shall be converted, and I will heal them." (D&C 112:13) This woman then had the faith sufficient to move forward, holding onto the promise that the person she had sorrowed for would one day become clean again.

Another woman, as she struggled with knowing how to deal with her father who had become involved in an adulterous relationship, was told in a priesthood blessing that she would be as a "warrior with a sword" in her dealings with him. She came to see that during times of interaction, the "sword" became the words of truth her father needed to hear. Though her father became angry at her since "the guilty taketh the truth to be hard," (1 Nephi 16:2) she could move forward knowing that she would be able to "speak the thoughts that I shall put into your hearts and you shall not be confounded before men. For it shall be given you in the very hour, yea, in the very moment, what ye shall say." (D&C 100:5-6) Time and time again, as this woman interacted with her father, she was given inspired words, both written and verbal, to say to him. She knew the messages were sent from the Lord to begin to counteract her father's rationalizations for sin for "I, the Lord, am not to be mocked in these last days." (D&C 63:58)

Another woman, who watched a daughter stray through infidelity, described the difficulty of watching this happen as a mother and the resulting pain she felt because of it. "The hurt I felt for my child made me actually hurt physically. My heart hurt," she said. She felt as Nephi did as he witnessed the sins of his people with her heart "swollen with sorrow." (Helaman 7:6) Comfort was given to this woman one day as she attended the temple. As she participated in a session, a peaceful reassurance came into her mind as she thought about her straying child. "Be patient," she was told. As this divine directive came, she implicitly sensed that through time and through patience those things that she desired—the repentance and healing of her daughter—would come to pass. Although she still had to hold on in faith, she now had an anchor to sustain her through the difficulties that would follow until her daughter did return to the fold.

The Lord will give each person struggling with the repercussions of infidelity the necessary insights, wisdom and direction to know how to deal with whatever befalls them because of another's transgressions. "Inasmuch as they are faithful unto me, it shall be made known unto them what they shall do," He promises us. (D&C 52:4)

When Persecution Comes to the Innocent

After Alma the Elder heard the words of the prophet Abinadi, he made the necessary changes in his life, began to repent and started living righteously. Many others followed his example. Not long after this, however, Amulon, someone with whom Alma had associated with as a high priest in the court of the wicked King Noah, was put in a position of power and authority over Alma and his people and he "began to persecute" them. (Mosiah 24:8) Alma had been living righteously; his people had been living righteously. Yet persecution still came to them because of the unrighteous actions of another. The burdens they were called upon to carry were heavy and unjustly placed upon them.

In cases of infidelity, similar situations arise with innocent parties who have tried to remain true to marriage covenants. They are inevitably persecuted by those who are living in sin. They become subjected to verbal attacks, injustices or other wicked designs put in motion against them. One such man, Rick, worked with his boss for several years. Rick had become a close friend of his boss and they often spent time together outside the office with their wives. As they continued this type of association, unbeknownst to Rick his boss began having an affair with his wife.

For over two years Rick's wife and boss lied to him as they spent trips, lunches and late nights together. Only when Rick discovered the affair did they admit to the double lives they had been leading. They were not in the least sorry for what they had done but became bitter and angry toward Rick. They immediately began blaming Rick for their affair, stating their actions had been justified because of the problems he had created in his marriage. They told him that he was incapable of overcoming his problems, problems he'd had for "years," and that he had left his wife unhappy and unfulfilled and therefore "open" to any man who would give her the attention she needed. They also claimed that he was manipulative and deceitful.

Because Rick couldn't immediately leave his job after discovering this betrayal, he became subjected to bitter verbal attacks from both his wife and his boss. As they made the choice to break up their marriages and move toward a marriage together, the persecution became even more intense. They began to make up lies and stories about dark deeds Rick had supposedly done and then twisted many of his past deeds to make them appear as if things were amiss. They told others, some who believed them, the lies and story about his supposed indiscretions. Some turned away from Rick although a few saw through the lies and remained friends.

As Rick went through these trials, leaving his job was not an immediate option unless he suffered grave financial loss. He had to continue working, being subjected to this type of persecution, before he could find another job and move away from them. Rick only survived emotionally by doing those things the people of Alma had done. "So great were there afflictions," the scriptures state, "that they began to cry mightily to God." (Mosiah 24:10)

Those prayers of desperation were heard. "The voice of the Lord came to them in their afflictions, saying: Lift up your heads and be of good comfort, for I know of the covenant which ye have made unto me; and I will covenant with my people and deliver them out of bondage. ...This will I do that ye may stand as witnesses for me...that I, the Lord God, do visit my people in their afflictions." (Mosiah 24:13-14) Although this did not happen immediately, "the Lord did strengthen them that they did submit cheerfully and with patience to all the will of the Lord." (Mosiah 24:15)

This is what Rick had to do. He had to turn to the Lord to help lift the heavy burdens and intense persecution unjustly placed upon him. He felt the Lord's strength and comfort sustain him as he faced those who hated and condemned him. He was blessed with others around him who saw the situation for what it was. He was assured through priesthood blessings that he was in the Lord's hands and that the Lord would never forget his faithfulness. As it was with the people of Alma, so great was Rick's faith and patience in enduring what he'd been called to pass through that the Lord soon delivered him from these trying circumstances by opening up another career path for him.

Although those who have remained faithful may be made to suffer "all manner of accusations" (D&C 122:6) or be "greatly oppressed and afflicted by wicked men," (D&C 109:48) those persons can trust that through time and through faith, the Lord will "go with them and deliver them out of bondage." (Mosiah 24:17) The Lord will, in "his time…cut off those wicked, unfaithful and unjust stewards" who persecute them. (D&C 101:90) As they are "faithful in Christ," the Savior will lift, comfort and guide them, giving them the spiritual sustenance needed to endure what others will inflict upon them because of their wickedness. (Moroni 9:25) As Jacob promises in the *Book of Mormon,* "Look unto God with firmness of mind, and pray unto him with exceeding faith, and he will console you in your afflictions, and he will plead your cause, and send down justice upon those who seek your destruction." (Jacob 3:1)

6

If a Spouse Returns to a Marriage

If a straying partner chooses to come back to a marriage and the committed spouse is willing to accept that person back, the only way for the marriage to return to any degree of wholeness is through the sustaining strength of our Lord and Savior, Jesus Christ. The Savior is the key—the *only* key. Only He can provide the in-depth healing needed in a relationship where infidelity has occurred.

Only the Savior can provide the sustenance, love, healing and strength necessary for the one who has been wronged to move forward toward forgiveness. As the Lord told one woman in a priesthood blessing who struggled to forgive her husband of his sexual sins, "The Lord is there to comfort and console you. Every tear that falls on your pillow and every prayer, He feels perfectly. He knows the burdens of others' sins and has carried them as well. He will help you carry these burdens." This woman knew that turning to the Savior during times of intense hardship, when she could not handle the pain and anguish she was experiencing, became the only way she could move forward and even attempt to rebuild her marriage.

When a partner does return to a marriage, it's as if there is a complete starting over. The old marriage and covenants are invalid. This starting over is a painful process of rebuilding and endurance—endurance to overcome the behaviors and thought patterns that led a partner astray, endurance to overcome the marital problems that have been exacerbated and blown out of proportion because of a partner's sins, and endurance to forgive the grievances that have and will continue to come as a spouse attempts but cannot immediately make necessary life and heart changes.

Only those who have the sustaining strength of the Savior will make it through these dark days of confusion and uncertainty. Only those who cast their burdens at the feet of the Savior will find any degree of forgiveness to live again with a partner who has betrayed them. Only those blessed with the necessary faith and hope will have the fortitude to overcome the contention and hardships a straying partner will inevitably bring into a relationship.

This sustaining power that comes from the Lord can be illustrated from an experience in *The Worth of a Soul* by Steven A. Cramer. He tells of his wife's suffering through his repentance process because of his adultery. He stated:

> [One] can easily imagine the agony that I caused [my wife] when I returned home with my confession. After standing by me...I had finally betrayed her in the worst way possible. Yet, her great spirit was able to look beyond her pain toward choosing the right. ...Her utmost desire in working through this situation was to be in harmony with the Lord's will for the family. She felt that whatever that meant, whether it was a divorce or still further forgiveness, her duty was to find his will and do it.
> (p. 35)

His wife felt directed by the Lord to stay with him but for two full years the family endured what he called "the buffetings of Satan" as they grappled with the consequences of his sins—his continuing anger, impatience and frustration with them. He continues:

The Lord provided a solution to our problem
by blessing my wife with the ability to borrow His
love and patience and forgiveness. ...My deliberate
disobedience to His law required me to suffer so that
I might find my way to repentance, but she deserved
a buffer—a sustaining strength to endure a trial that
would quickly surpass her natural strength. (p. 74)

The Lord did bless his wife with the strength and
fortitude necessary to deal with the difficulties that arose and the
burdens placed unfairly upon her. This strength came as a very
real and tangible gift that became known some time later after
peace and harmony once again began to be established in their
home. Steven A. Cramer said regarding this time:

Suddenly the harmony disappeared.
...Suddenly my wife was easily offended. She
would lose patience with me over little things. After
holding on and being so wonderful during those two
long years, ...suddenly she fell apart. She seemed to
have lost her ability to cope with even the smallest
stress.

His wife talked about these changes in her journal. She
wrote:

I had entered a period of depression unlike
any I had ever experienced before. It was really
awful. For about two weeks all I could do was lie on
the couch and brood and wonder what I should be
doing. I couldn't even organize my thoughts or
formulate any plans for keeping the house, etc.
Finally I got on my knees and asked the
Lord, "WHY?" What was happening to me? As I
pled for understanding, it was given to me. I was
told that all through the trials and adversity of my
husband's excommunication and subsequent
buffeting by Satan I had been given extra help from

45

beyond the veil, strength and power to endure that were more than my own ability.

I was told that now that the Lord had healed [my husband], the endowment was no longer proper. Now it was up to me to learn to adjust and to grow with him—to improve myself along with him. I was told that the "extra" help had been withdrawn from me, and now I needed to readjust and gain control and strength through my own efforts, with the continued help of the Lord. (p. 76)

This type of sustenance will only come from the Savior. Even if a returning spouse is trying to make necessary changes for a relationship to heal, true healing must still be centered on the Savior. This point was brought home to one woman, Angie, who dealt with the repercussions of her husband's unfaithfulness. As her husband tried to repent, she could see him slowly changing and beginning to take those first steps toward rebuilding their relationship. She would ask him, "Are you really changing? Are you committed to our relationship? Will you ever do those things again?" He would assure her that yes, he was changing and no, he wouldn't sin again. Again and again he spoke of his recommitment to her; again and again he would reassure that he was on the right path toward repentance.

But when we were first married, you made those same types of promises and you didn't keep them, Angie would think, not finding any solace or comfort from her husband's words or behavior. She could not move forward in their relationship because of her deep misgivings. Bitterness and hurt welled up inside her and it became impossible for her to get beyond those feelings.

One day as she was listening to music about the Savior and her thoughts centered on Him, a profound impression came into her mind. Angie knew, in those few moments of divine inspiration, that she had been attempting to get the healing she needed from her relationship—from seeing her husband's changes and becoming certain of his recommitment to their marriage. She suddenly knew what she'd been searching for could not work because she was looking to an outside source to heal what only the Savior could heal. Angie understood that she needed to heal *first* with the Savior and then the outside healing could follow. She further understood that whether or not ultimate healing occurred in their relationship, she could still be whole and move forward with her life, with or without her husband.

This idea was later confirmed in a priesthood blessing to her. She was told, "The Savior knows all of your emotional needs and all of your desires. He can fulfill all of them. You will come to understand how He is perfect in this way." As Angie began to center her life on the Savior and His unconditional love and acceptance of her, as she tapped into His strength and found solace in His peace, she no longer needed outside reinforcement through her husband or through their relationship for her healing. No matter what her husband's choices were or continued to be, she knew she could become whole because she had centered her heart on the only sure foundation, Jesus Christ.

Forgiveness into the Eternities

Although the Lord tells us that we must forgive, that the greater sin lies with us if we cannot forgive those who have trespassed against us, (D&C 64:9) forgiveness of a straying spouse has to be a process we learn and grow with and strive to reach just as we strive to reach perfection. Forgiveness for the grievous wrongs done by an unfaithful spouse will not happen all at once. Forgiveness will only be achieved through time and through a willing heart. Forgiveness will ultimately come about as a gift from our Savior whose capacity to forgive far outreaches our own. The process of forgiveness can begin, however, solely with the willingness to *try* to forgive.

One woman told of her experiences with her unfaithful husband. She had accepted him back after his affair with another woman so they could try to work on becoming a forever family once again. She continued on with their tempestuous marriage, working through their continuing problems and contention, only to discover her husband had begun lying to her again and was continuing his affair. Again they separated and started separate lives until her husband returned to her once more, begging her forgiveness and asking for a second chance. With a heavy heart and much misgiving, knowing she was doing this "only for the children," she accepted him back and began trying to rebuild their shattered relationship once again.

Although her husband truly began to make the necessary life changes this time, she found she could hardly forgive him. The distrust and the wounds were too deep and too painful to be overcome. She did not know how she would ever be able to forgive her husband's trespasses against her.

This woman had the opportunity to counsel with a loving General Authority at that time. He told her, "You need to understand that forgiveness for something like this might have to extend even into the eternities." Her heart swelled with relief with this statement. She could begin once more to *try* to move forward, knowing that she hoped to forgive her husband but that this process might last through to the eternities. She knew it was her willingness, not necessarily the completed task, which was needed.

If a Spouse Does Not Return to a Marriage

As the keys to healing a wounded relationship are found in the Savior, so are the keys to healing a wounded heart of one who is left alone following infidelity. Only those who have suffered through the unfaithfulness of a spouse can begin to understand the depth of pain and anguish caused by a betrayal. One woman told another, "As I saw you suffer through what you were going through [because of her husband's betrayal], I would cry buckets of tears for you. Even then, I never knew how hard it was until I had to go through it myself."

A mother who watched the pain of a daughter left alone after her husband's infidelity described the pain this way. "I lost a son-in-law to death (after a rollover accident) and I lost a son-in-law to divorce (due to his infidelity). The divorce was by far harder."

Although others cannot completely understand the pain of a betrayal, there is One who understands the extent to which we grieve—the very depths of our sorrow—when we are betrayed by someone we love. "The Lord cries with you," one woman was told in a priesthood blessing after the unfaithfulness of her husband. "This trial that came to you was not necessary to humble or refine you but happened because of another person's choices." The Lord then reassured this woman, as He does to all, that He would walk with her every step of the way through this trial and through the remainder of her life. "The Lord is servant to all," He reminded her. "Even though He is the greatest of all, He is servant to all. Therefore, He desires to help you." He further promised her, "The Lord *never* forgets the faithful." As with all things, the Savior is the key—the absolute *only* key—to lasting healing and wholeness.

The Wounds of the Children

The prophet Jacob in the *Book of Mormon* warns spouses that have betrayed their partners to "remember your children, how that ye have grieved their hearts because of the example that ye have set before them; and also remember that ye may, because of your filthiness, bring your children unto destruction, and their sins be heaped upon your heads at the last day." (Jacob 3:10) Children of straying spouses, whether those spouses will be leaving the marriage or not, are deeply affected by the sins of a parent. Not only are they influenced by the spirit that is brought into their homes, their security and feelings of safety are shattered by those things that have happened to them and around them.

One young girl, who was not aware that her father had betrayed her mother, still felt deeply the tension in their home. As she was still in her formative years, she could not vocalize the troubled feelings of uprootedness and abandonment she felt. As she dealt with these emotions, she began pulling out her eyelashes in a troubled behavior pattern—an outward indication that showed her inward turmoil. This habit continued through the years the problems remained in their home.

Some younger children in similar situations may begin wetting the bed whereas they haven't for some time. Some don't sleep well or have nightmares. Some cry and fight more or are more demanding of attention. Many children begin to struggle in school, become withdrawn or unsettled, and often look to friends or others outside the home for needed security. Some children are influenced by the destructive forces in the home and begin to engage in their own wicked behaviors. Often children's courses of wickedness are directly related to their parents' wicked behavior.

One man, looking back over his teenage years of sin and rebellion, realized that the mistakes he now regretted from his past occurred during the time his father was having an affair. Although this man accepted responsibility for his actions, he came to believe he had been influenced by the spirit his father brought into their home. In *The Worth of a Soul,* Steven A. Cramer describes an experience that illustrates this idea further. He told of the time when, while engaging in sinful behaviors, he used his daughter's bed to sleep during the day because of his nightly shifts at work. He then describes what happened:

> During the awful period when I had abandoned myself to pornography without restraint, I had a terrible dream about my nine-year-old daughter whose bed I used. I dreamed I had slipped over the edge of a precipice of a very deep chasm. As I was clinging to the cliff, this nine-year-old daughter came running to help me. But she also slipped and fell past me into the chasm toward certain death. In dumbfounded terror I screamed her name as I helplessly watched her fall. As her body fell further and further from my sight, I could hear her calling to me, "I love you, Dad. ...I love you, Dad."
>
> I awoke from the dream in a cold sweat. I could not go back to sleep. That dream had meaning, I was certain, but what could it mean? Were we going to lose her with a premature death? Was she going to fall away from the Church as I had?

As he discussed this dream with his wife, the meaning of the dream became clear:

> My wife pointed out that my daughter's fall was related to my fall. If I had not been in jeopardy, she would not have perished. My wife then confided to me that for some time this young daughter had complained of feeling evil spirits who were "putting bad thoughts" in her mind, especially when she was trying to go to sleep. Among other things, they told her not to pray, not to read the scriptures, and not to believe her teachers at church. The torment was so persistent and she was so often frightened that she frequently had to leave her bed and join my wife in

our bedroom to feel safe again. Often she was awakened by terrifying dreams.

The bond between her peril and mine was obvious. I realized that the evil influence of [my behaviors] lingered. (p. 79)

After getting this daughter a special priesthood blessing and because of his choice not to sleep in her room anymore, she was no longer troubled as deeply by these evil influences.

As children struggle through the trauma that infidelity inevitably brings, their spiritual wholeness needs to be safeguarded as much as an injured spouse's needs to be. Although it takes effort to look past inward turmoil and pain, one must reach out in loving awareness to these children and help them through the turbulent times. Prayer and scripture reading are vital. Children should also receive priesthood blessings of strength, comfort and protection. They, too, are going through a painful time and need to be carefully safeguarded.

7

Relying on the Savior

As I struggled through the uncertainty and difficulty of knowing how to help my friend Rebecca through the process of her husband's infidelity, I found comfort from the words of a special priesthood blessing I received which essentially said: "The Lord sheds many tears as he knows you feel hurt for those around you who have chosen to lead lives that are not pleasing to the Lord. He knows your heart and cries with you. But remember, the Savior loves each of his children infinitely more than we, as brothers and sisters, love our brothers and sisters. He knows perfectly what each child needs. As you rely upon the One who has paid the price for all sins, for all disloyalties, for all lying, for all the bad, as you rely upon Him and ask Him how to deal with each individual that you come in contact with in your life, you will know what to do for each person."

Each of us must in turn rely upon this One who has "paid the price for all sins, for all disloyalties" to know what to do in all cases pertaining to infidelity. For those who need to tap into the power and strength of the Savior, I would like to share the keys I've found necessary to maintaining a life centered on Christ, especially through times of spiritual turbulence.

Prayer

Let prayer become a lifeline. Share with the Lord *everything*—hurts, sorrows, pains, fears, uncertainties, doubts, confusion, stresses—*everything*. Share with Him spiritual yearnings and desires. Let hearts be drawn out in prayer to Him always. He desires and wants to be our best and closest friend. Also, never cease praying for those lost in sin because...

> ...for unto such ye shall continue to minister; for ye know not but what they will return and repent, and come unto me with full purpose of heart, and I shall heal them; and ye shall be the means of bringing salvation unto them. (3 Nephi 18:32)

Scriptures

Feast upon the scriptures daily, not just ten or fifteen minutes but a half hour *at least.* Do not miss out on this necessary spiritual nourishment—*ever.* It is essential for survival. Even if a mind is filled with confusion and darkness because of life circumstances, the very act of letting eyes rest on the words will bring an element of strength, protection and comfort. Searching scriptures will yield needed answers that have never been previously discovered. Often insights on how to deal with everything happening will be revealed. For any dealing with the contention, persecution and misjudgment that will be a part of life because of another's sins, our Savior will fill an empty bucket with strength, knowledge and comfort that will help incrementally in progress toward healing and wholeness.

Relinquishment

Each must make an everlasting promise to the Lord that, as the Savior did, he or she will "suffer the will of the father in all things." (3 Nephi 11:11) It takes a great deal of faith and determination to do whatever will be required of the Lord but doing everything the Lord's way is the only key to survival. If the Lord wants someone to stay in a broken relationship, then stay—knowing that He will help that person see and understand the reasons He has asked him or her to do so even if that relationship does not ultimately work out. If the Lord wants a person to leave a relationship, then leave. He has meaning and purpose to each life and promises that "all things shall work together for your good." (D&C 90:24) He has the ordained power to make this happen.

If the Lord desires us to do anything, remember He does only that which will work for our good—that which will be for our optimal benefit, that which will help us, strengthen us, give us growth, and help us realize the greatest amount of blessings possible at the best times possible. As hard is it may be to accept the Lord's will at difficult junctures in life, we cannot hesitate to seek to do that which He asks. We must trust that He has a path to take that will lead to eternal happiness and that one day perfect justice and restitution will be meted out for all inequities suffered in this life. "Forget not his benefits," we are reminded in Psalms. "The Lord...redeemeth thy life from destruction" and "crowneth thee with lovingkindness and tender mercies." (Psalm 103:4) The Lord will never forget the pains and afflictions of His suffering children but is there to help, strengthen, comfort and heal them.

Priesthood Blessings

Not all dispensations have been blessed like ours with the fullness of the priesthood to rely upon. Priesthood blessings are an invaluable source from which to receive comfort, direction, guidance, solace, strength, insights and intimate, personal revelation. This is truly a priceless gift that the Lord has allowed us to have at this time. We must use it. We must call upon those who are willing and worthy to be the Lord's mouthpiece. We must rely on the promises given through the

Spirit and then follow the directives given. Blessing upon blessing will come, line upon line of understanding and knowledge will be given as the priesthood is used for strength, guidance, and direction.

Remember that the priesthood is called the "Holy Order after the Son of God" because it is used in the similitude of how we rely upon our Savior. When we call upon it, we are asking for the Lord's strength and guidance, not for a mortal's strength and guidance. Calling upon it is therefore a sign of faith, not a sign of weakness. One woman, who felt she had to get blessing after blessing to keep her head afloat during her difficult trials after her husband's infidelity, felt that this constant asking for priesthood blessings showed a lack of faith on her part. However, the Lord told her that He did not see it that way—that her calling upon His strength in this way was not a sign of weakness but a sign of faith. He admonished her that she could draw as much water from this never-ending well to quench her thirsty soul as she needed.

Temple Attendance

Although sometimes attending the temple seems like it may sap strength and energy during difficult times, attending the temple will inevitably strengthen souls in ways that cannot be seen. Attending the temple regularly helps a heart become more centered on the Lord, His guidance and His strength. Often individuals who attend the temple will become more aware of those on the other side of the veil who are willing to help, support and strengthen them in their difficult burdens. The Lord promises those who go to the temple that they will be "armed with [his] power," that "his glory [will] be round about them," and that His angels will have "charge over them." (D&C 109:22)

It is wise to keep names of suffering family members on the prayer roll. Many times the faith of others can carry us when we don't have the necessary faith or strength to move forward ourselves. Remember also that the spirit of the temple can often attend us in our homes after we leave that sacred place to help us better deal with challenging difficulties.

"The Battle is not Yours but God's" (2 Chronicles 20:15)

Many do not have the happy ending of Rebecca's story in the "Foreword" of this book where she, along with her husband, were able to endure in faith and rebuild their marriage. Today an extensive amount of time has passed since these incidents and her husband is "better than ever." He has truly "brought forth fruits meet for repentance" (Alma 13:13) in his life and these fruits have brought her and her children much joy and stability. "Because…the Spirit of the Lord Omnipotent wrought a mighty change in [him], or in [his] heart…[he has] no more disposition to do evil, but to do good continually." (Mosiah 5:2)

Although many others do not have the same experience in terms of healing their marriages, they can have similar blessings in terms of the spiritual healing and wholeness Rebecca experienced. They, as she has done, may learn to center their lives on Christ and trust that He loves them, watches over them and cares for them, whatever difficult circumstances they are called to go through. They can understand that the Savior is aware of every trial they will face and have faced and that He will continue to share those trials with them. They can come to realize that the Savior will never leave them alone or comfortless. (John 14:18) They can rest assured that the burdens that have come into their lives, not because of the Savior's will but because of another's sins, will be compensated for one day. They can move forward with the knowledge that the Savior will give them the necessary strength to carry these burdens and ultimately make these burdens light. They can come to know with certainty that as they plug into the Savior's power and receive of His strength, love, and ability to serve, they will receive the capacity to love and serve those around them who are suffering, as well.

Furthermore, they can come to testify that the healing power of the Savior is real and that He will provide healing to them as needed. They can come to understand that when they have none of their own strength left to carry them, the Savior will extend His arm, upholding and uplifting them until they are ready to move forward again. They can come to learn that the Savior will tenderly work with their weaknesses and that as He makes their weaknesses become known, He will lead them step by gentle step toward wholeness. As He does this, they will come to taste of His goodness—His everlasting kindness, mercy, and patience with them. They can move forward forever assured that the Lord will guide, direct and counsel as needed. They can realize with certainty that, if they endure their trials well, that "God shall exalt [them] on high" and "[they] shall triumph over all [their] foes." (D&C 121:8)

Most importantly, they will come to understand that there is One who has already faced and gone through every experience of their lives and as He walks them through these experiences once again, they will never be alone. They will always have the Lord's unconditional love to buoy and carry them. They can know, without a doubt, that He is their great, loving, Eternal Friend.

"They Fell Away Into Forbidden Paths"
(1 Nephi 8:28):

DEALING WITH THOSE BOUND BY THE SIN OF INFIDELITY

1

"My Soul is Rent with Anguish Because of You"
(1 Nephi 17:47)

Some of the greatest pain I have ever witnessed, besides the suffering of those who have felt the immense pain of a betrayal, was the suffering and anguish of a mother struggling over the decisions of a wayward daughter. Only a few short years after this daughter's temple sealing, she had participated in an adulterous affair which destroyed her marriage, traumatized her two young children, and sent rippling effects of shock, pain and hurt throughout the remainder of her extended family. This daughter, like the rest of her family, had been raised in the Church. She had been taught the truth and seemed to be a valiant and strong spirit. Her brothers had served missions and married in the temple. She and each of her sisters had married in the temple, as well. They had all started families of their own.

This daughter had seemed to have it all. She had a kind, caring, conscientious husband who helped often with both the housework and the care of the children. They were financially stable, lived in a beautiful home, and had money for all the "extras." Other siblings often envied their lifestyle of relative ease and prosperity.

After a few years of married life, however, there seemed to be a slow and gradual change in this once-happy union. Although secure financially, an emotional distance between this woman and her husband seemed to emerge. Contention and

61

bickering soon followed, contention not hidden from family members. This woman began to spend many untold hours outside her home, leaving her children in the care of others. Her home, which had always been carefully cared for, soon showed signs of neglect.

Shortly after the birth of this woman's second child, her husband came to find out that this woman had been having an affair with her boss at work. Not only did he have to deal with the feelings of betrayal and hurt that resulted from this knowledge, he had to deal with the emotional devastation of discovering that their second child was not his. He watched in dismay as his once-peaceful lifestyle crumbled about him. This woman shortly after married her boss and the child her husband thought had been his was taken away from him completely.

Although the knowledge of this affair affected each and every member of this couple's extended family, the pain seemed to be most deeply and lastingly felt by this woman's mother. She cried and ached with an intensity she had never before felt; her prayers became fervent, pleading and desperate. She had to watch with unceasing concern and anguish as her daughter continued on in sin.

As this mother witnessed the destructive choices her daughter made, she became almost immobilized by grief. She often sobbed and spent many sleepless nights in painful agonizing. What had gone wrong? Why had her daughter strayed? Why did she continue to make these bad choices? What, if anything, had she as a mother done in the past that might have contributed to her daughter's behavior? Did she bear any of the responsibility for what had happened and if she did, what was she to do about it? She agonized further over what would eventually happen to her grandchildren. Because they were still in their formative years, she worried about the types of influences they had in their home. What was her responsibility to them since she loved them as if they were her own? How could she help them? How could she help her daughter see what she was doing and help her look past her all-consuming selfishness to their needs?

Most of all, what could she do or say to help this daughter return to the fold, to help her come back to the Savior and completely repent of all the evil and darkness that had entered her life? She wanted to be able to help her daughter see the magnitude and depth of her sins and help her overcome the rationalizations that had become rampant and pervasive in her thinking. She wanted her daughter to be able to admit to all the lies she had told to everyone, lies that in her daughter's mind had been fed and cultivated for so long they had now become truth. She wanted this daughter to have the courage and determination to be able to confess the extent of her deception so she could begin to move forward toward the healing she desperately needed. Would her prayers of faith and pleading have any impact on her daughter's welfare?

These days became times of great struggle and searching, times when this mother felt the deepest heartache and pain she had ever felt in her life. She had lost a brother and her mother to death but she confided to a friend one day that she felt like it might have been easier to lose this daughter to death rather than having lost her to something such as this. With death, there still remained the hope of a joyful reunion. But how could she ever be certain of her daughter's joyful return with the decisions she continued to make?

This woman wanted to understand what it was that had brought her daughter down to the depths of sin she'd reached — and reached relatively quickly. She wanted to comprehend the effects and cycles of sin so that she, too, could help her daughter combat the lies and deceptions she'd used to justify sinful behavior.

More than anything, this woman wanted to help her daughter find her way back to the Savior so with His help she could find the necessary insights to begin the long road toward repentance. She knew that her daughter's true healing would only come through Him, that hope, faith, comfort, peace and lasting happiness would only come as gifts from the One who had already paid the price for all of her daughter's sins.

As this mother struggled dealing with this situation, she knew she had to turn to the Lord to help her gain whatever insights she needed to continue forward. The Savior became her only solace. She grasped for any hope or anchor through priesthood blessings and through the scriptures that might help her. She sought desperately for any personal revelation that would sustain her through the trials of the continued darkness she still saw in her daughter's life. She would often plead for the Lord's strength to carry on with her own life, which seemed nearly impossible with the added burdens she now carried.

Many who go through a similar experience with a wayward son or daughter of God seem to have these same types of questions and these same types of struggles. They want and desperately need to comprehend in a small way what has happened to someone who has fallen away into "forbidden paths." (1 Nephi 8:28) They want to know what they can do to help that person find the Savior once again and through His healing power become whole and clean. They want to understand the process that will help lead that person through the necessary steps of repentance and give him or her the needed strength, hope, and faith to let go of the darkness and return to the light.

This section addresses the concerns of those who are dealing with a wayward husband or wife, brother or sister, other relative, friend or associate who has been unfaithful. Struggles involving sinning parties may bring about some of the deepest trials, anguish and pain a person might ever have to go through in this life. As with anything, hope and true strength in dealing with these issues must come from the Savior who "knoweth the weakness of man and how to succor them who are tempted." (D&C 62:1) It is only through Him, who has "descended below all things," (D&C 88:6) that we can find the capacity to cope with others for whom we feel an eternal concern. He is our one and only true source of love, light, peace, truth and lasting happiness. He is the only one who can fully comprehend the feelings and attitudes of both the sinner and the ones who have been wronged and lead them respectively back to forgiveness and healing.

2

"They Did Yield Themselves Unto the Power of Satan" (3 Nephi 7:5)

"Why do you think the prophets are reminding us of our sacred duty to...protect the home and family?" Joanne B. Doxey once asked. "Because it is against the home and family that Satan has aimed his greatest efforts to destroy, *and far too many sheep are wandering or being enticed away out of the fold, and wolves lie in wait to devour the flock.*" (*Ensign*, Nov. 1987, italics added) Evidence of Satan's destruction and his attacks against the family can be found in the fact that many choice sons and daughters of God, some who have married in the temple and have made sacred eternal covenants, are participating in the sin of infidelity. Adultery, fornication, homosexuality and all their attendant sins have become rampant and are growing in ever increasing numbers both within and without the Church.

Those who love these choice sons and daughters of God often watch in amazement as those persons they care for get "enticed away out of the flock"—as they buy into Satan's lies and intricate deceptions used to justify sinful behaviors. Many stand helplessly by as they watch these sons and daughters give heed to the words of those in the "great and spacious building," (1 Nephi 8:26) those who would entice them to sin with their "lying and craftiness" (Alma 12:3) and "flattering words." (Mosiah 11:7)

Some of the greatest pain we can ever experience comes from watching the process of sin and its devastating effects on loved ones and their families. Even the Savior expressed this great anguish as He visited the Nephites after His ascension into heaven. "Jesus groaned within himself," the scriptures tell us, "and said: Father, *I am troubled* because of the wickedness of the people of the house of Israel." (3 Nephi 17:14, italics added)

To help deal with the devastation of knowing someone lost in sin, we first must understand what happens to those who have become vulnerable and then participate in sin. We must come to see some of the behaviors and weaknesses that contribute to this vulnerability. We also must study the general attitudes adopted and the processes these people go through in their spiral downward, a spiral which continues until a thorough repentance is made or until "the cup of their iniquity is full." (D&C 101:11)

Secondly, we must explore ways in which we can offer help to those lost in sin and in turn find our own peace and comfort in dealing with these situations. We must understand the point in which we, after all we can do, must "trust" sinning parties "unto the Lord." (Alma 19:23) Lastly, we must gain insights into the steps of repentance that will help a loved one find the way back to the Savior. We must be willing to counsel and help them understand principles that in our own lives are tried and true. Even if those we love are unwilling or do not accept our efforts or counsel, we must, through our "diligence, faithfulness, and the prayers of faith," find "victory" (D&C 103:36)—that is, we must exercise our faith and prayers in their behalf so that they will some day make their way back to the Savior, who is the mainstream of all peace, comfort, joy and lasting happiness. Then and only then will the ones we love become whole again. Then and only then will the ones we love find the happiness they have been searching for.

3

"Thou Shalt Not Commit Adultery...Nor Do Anything Like Unto It" (D&C 59:6)

I remember sitting in a room one day watching one of my sons, who was a little over a year and a half at the time, play. I felt such a surge of love for him as I studied him, as I saw his head bent over what he was doing, as I heard the happy sounds he made as he enjoyed this time. As I sat there for those few moments watching him, I felt a feeling of deep gratitude that I'd been given the opportunity to have him and raise him. I marveled at his life. I marveled that his little body had been created by my husband and me and now housed his precious spirit. As I pondered this, it literally amazed me to realize that this beautiful little boy and his resulting life had come about because of one sacred act. As I thought and pondered on the wonder of this further, the Lord whispered to my mind, "That is why there are such strict laws as to govern its use [the use of these life-giving powers]."

For the first time I think I glimpsed more fully the seriousness of the procreative act and why the Lord has given such strict laws and commandments to govern its use. The ability to create someone's life is inherent in that power, an ability the Lord does not want us to tamper with in any way. The Lord loves His children. He wants what is best for them. The effects of tampering with this power are not only serious for the offenders but hold far-reaching negative consequences for their families and extended families, as well. That is why the

Lord warns us over and over through scriptures, latter-day prophets and leaders of the painful repercussions and consequences that arise from misuse of these sacred powers.

The two most grievous sins that the Lord has delineated for us—besides the unpardonable sin of "[denying] the Holy Ghost when it once has had place in you" (Alma 39:6)—involve the misuse of life-giving and life-taking powers. The first sin delineated is murder, or the taking of life, and the second sin mentioned is adultery or sexual immorality, tampering with the powers that give life. Alma told his wayward son, Corianton, who had forsaken his ministry to go over into the land of Siron after the harlot Isabel, "Know ye not, my son, that these [sexual sins] are an abomination in the sight of the Lord; yea, most abominable above all sins save it be the shedding of innocent blood or denying the Holy Ghost?" (Alma 39:5)

It is little wonder that we hear warnings again and again about the serious repercussions of sexual immorality. Elder Richard G. Scott described these powers and the resulting consequences of their misuse in the *Ensign*. He said:

> Intimate acts are forbidden by the Lord outside of marriage because they undermine His purposes. When experienced any other way, they are against His will. They cause serious emotional and spiritual harm. It causes powerful physical and emotional stimulation. In time that creates an unquenchable appetite that drives the offender to ever more serious sin. It engenders selfishness and can produce aggressive acts such as brutality, abortion, sexual abuse, and violent crime. Such stimulation can lead to acts of homosexuality, and they are evil and absolutely wrong. Sexual transgression would...sap your spiritual strength, undermine your faith in Jesus Christ, and frustrate your ability to serve him. (Nov. 1994)

Many in the Church are often amazed by the fact that some who have known and been taught the seriousness of sexual immorality would go against the will of the Lord and abuse these sacred procreative powers. Many are astounded by the fact that these choice sons and daughters, who do "not sin ignorantly, for they [know] the will of God concerning them," (3 Nephi 6:18) have been swayed by the temptations and whisperings of Satan. Through Satan's power, lies and deceit, they somehow come to believe their abuse of these powers is justified. "Others will he pacify, and lull them away into carnal security, that they will say: All is well in Zion," the scriptures tell us. (2 Nephi 28:21)

"We will need greater spirituality to perceive all the forms of evil and greater strength to resist it," President James E. Faust once told us. *(Ensign,* Nov. 1994) In other words, we need to come to understand the patterns and cycles of infidelity so that we may, in turn, gather the strength and fortitude to resist it. Those dealing with a wayward life of someone they love must come to "perceive all the forms of evil" so that they can begin to steer those they love toward the understanding of the seriousness of their transgressions, an understanding which will hopefully help transgressors begin the long journey toward repentance. With this understanding, those injured may begin to seek for personal healing from the pain of all that has happened to them and around them.

4

"Ye are Beginning to Labor in Sin" *(Jacob 2:5)*

The story of Lehi's family contains great insights into the cycle and downward process of what happens to those who sin. Ironically, the simple murmuring of Laman and Lemuel against their father ultimately led them to greater sin and "hardness of their hearts" (1 Nephi 2:18) until they were actually willing to commit murder and engage in wicked behaviors "full of mischief and subtlety." (2 Nephi 5:24)

It is interesting to study the cycles that occur as Laman and Lemuel persist in their wickedness. As time passes, their murmuring increases and their other sins grow in proportion, as well. Their hearts became more and more hardened with each sinful act. Although the Lord chastens them unto repentance many times, finally their hearts become so hardened, "like unto a flint," (2 Nephi 5:21) that He can no longer work with them.

For example, after a failed attempt to get the brass plates from Laban, Laman and Lemuel became angry. They "did speak many hard words" unto Nephi and Sam and "did smite [them] even with a rod." (1 Nephi 3:28) Although they saw an angel, who assured them that "the Lord will deliver Laban into your hands," their murmuring still continued. (1 Nephi 3:29-31) This cycle of murmuring and anger intensified. Not long afterward, as Nephi and his brothers traveled in the wilderness with Ishmael's family, Laman and Lemuel became angry with Nephi once again, insomuch that "they did lay their hands upon [him], for behold, they were exceedingly wroth, and they did bind [him] with cords, for they sought to take away [his] life, that they might leave [him] in the wilderness to be devoured by wild beasts." (1 Nephi 7:16) Through chastening words of some of the others, they became "sorrowful because of their wickedness, insomuch that they did bow down before [Nephi], and did plead with [him] that [he] would forgive them." (1 Nephi 7:20) Not long after this, however, Laman stirs Lemuel and others against Nephi once again, claiming Nephi is a liar and that "he tells us these things, and he worketh many things by his cunning arts, that he may deceive our eyes...to make himself a king and a ruler over us." (1 Nephi 16:37-38)

Time and time again this cycle occurs: Laman's and Lemuel's toying with sin—"they began to dance, and to sing, and to speak with much rudeness," (1 Nephi 18:9) their seeking Nephi's detriment—"Laman and Lemuel did take me and bind me with cords, and they did treat me with much hardness" (1 Nephi 18:11) and then their humbling, which leads them toward repentance. "My brethren began to see that the judgments of God were upon them, and that they must perish save that they should repent of their iniquities," Nephi said. (1 Nephi 18:15)

This cycle happened over and over until the time that Laman and Lemuel became so hardened in their ways and works that the Lord had to warn Nephi and his followers to depart from them because they "did seek to take away [Nephi's] life." (2 Nephi 5:2) Laman and Lemuel, because of their continuing transgression, were ultimately removed from the presence of the Lord. (2 Nephi 5:20)

A very similar cycle can occur with those who violate the law of chastity. Often it is the small acts, the simple habits and behaviors that can lead them to the greater sin of infidelity. The persistent small and simple acts in the "gray areas" can ultimately allow Satan to come in until he begins the downward process of destruction. Many who have once known the Savior ultimately cut themselves off from His influence.

Spencer W. Kimball once described this process and cycle of sin in the fable of a camel and his owner traveling across the desert. A terrible wind storm comes up and the camel begs for entrance into the traveler's tent. The owner at first refuses but ultimately acquiesces and then allows the camel's nose inside the tent. Soon the head, front quarters, torso and hind quarters follow, kicking the traveler out into the wind and storm.

> If a door is slightly ajar, [Satan] gets his toe in, and soon this is followed by his foot, then by his leg and his body and his head, and finally he is in all the way. ...Soon the conscience is stilled completely, the evil power has full sway, and the door to salvation is closed until a thorough repentance opens it again. (*The Miracle of Forgiveness*, p. 215)

The *Book of Mormon* also describes giving into temptation. "The temptations of the devil...blindeth the eyes, and hardeneth the hearts of the children of men, and leadeth them away into broad roads, that they perish and are lost." (1 Nephi 12:17) Elder Rulon G. Craven stated, "To blind the eyes is not to see or acknowledge the consequence of our actions. To harden the heart is to ignore or not be willing to accept counsel. To be led into the broad roads is to give in to worldly enticements and lose the influence of the Holy Spirit in our lives." (*Ensign*, May 1996)

The following are some of the things that can bring us downward, some of the simple behaviors that can become our undoing and lead to greater sins:

Pride, Love of Riches, and Costly Apparel

During his ministry, the prophet Jacob called together and taught his people in the temple after being "weighed down with much...desire and anxiety for the welfare of [their] souls" to warn them about their pride, love of riches and the wearing of costly apparel. (Jacob 2:3) He said, "Because some of you have obtained more abundantly than that of your brethren ye...wear stiff necks and high heads because of the costliness of your apparel, and persecute your brethren because ye suppose that ye are better than they." (Jacob 2:13) It is interesting to note that these sins had become the precursor to the abominations and whoredoms many of the people were beginning to practice.

Throughout the *Book of Mormon*, it is a recurrent theme that whenever people are ripening in sin, they often have problems with pride, their use of riches, and the wearing of "costly apparel." (See Alma 1:32 and Helaman 7:26) All three behaviors denote a preoccupation with self—with "glory and the vain things of the world," (Alma 60:32) things such as obtaining wealth solely for one's personal benefit, feeling greater than others because of this wealth and an obsession with the physical appearance and "the life of the body." (D&C 101:37)

Preoccupation with self can occur in many different forms and often creates a fertile breeding ground for Satan's lies and rationalizations that can lead one to further sin. For one woman, problems with infidelity occurred after she became obsessed with her body and figure. For a greater amount of her married life she had been very heavy. After losing a significant amount of weight, she began tanning frequently, buying clothes to show off her new figure, and going out in public more.

This preoccupation with her body turned to her detriment. She became vulnerable to those who gave her attention. Soon she began seeking outside associations,

associations which led her to places where the Spirit of the Lord could not reside. Not long after, she began having an affair and then simultaneous affairs, associations which came to tear apart her young family.

Not Doing the "Little" Things, Making "Little" Mistakes

One woman had the chance to talk to her father, who had been a stake president, about some of the people he had dealt with during his tenure in that stake calling. This woman questioned him about those he had worked with who had been lost in sin, many who had been taught and raised in the Church but had participated in infidelity or other forms of transgression. "What is it," she questioned her father, "that would make these people vulnerable to sin after all they know and after all they've been taught?"

Her father answered, "I believe people become vulnerable to sin when they stop doing the little things—when they stop attending their meetings, saying their prayers, reading their scriptures and paying their tithing. They become even more vulnerable when they begin to make little mistakes. When people begin showing weaknesses in these areas, it's like holding up a neon sign to Satan and saying, 'Look, I'm vulnerable and weak. Come and get me.'"

Neglecting to do the simple things that keep us on the strait and narrow path can become our undoing. Often as we begin to have lacks in the spiritual arena in our lives, it is much easier for things to go amiss in other areas. Small mistakes can then become bigger mistakes with disastrous eternal consequences.

Imbalance

Sadly, any type of imbalance that comes into our lives

can make us vulnerable to Satan for he knows when we are weak, exhausted or discouraged—times when we might be more open to his whisperings since we are not able to fight him as effectively. Imbalance can come from many different sources. Sometimes continued stresses which we cannot solve or eradicate, even stresses from everyday life which have not come about because of any sin or transgression, can cause the kind of imbalance which creates a breeding ground conducive to Satan's lies and deceptions.

One man struggled through several intense years of study as he tried to gain an education for his chosen profession. As he carried on with his church callings and helped in raising his young family, he worked many long, hard and wearing hours. Toward the end of his schooling, he met a woman who showed him much kindness and concern over the stresses he'd dealt with in his life. She sought him out to give him love, attention and caring. She showered him with adoration and praise. Soon her attentions turned to other physical advances.

Ultimately this man had an affair with her. The imbalances in his life contributed to his being enticed away from his family by someone who had preyed upon his vulnerabilities in moments of stress, weakness and exhaustion.

Imbalance in our lives can also occur from any kind of addiction, from the simple addiction to the caffeine in soft drinks to stronger addictions of alcohol or other substances. When we are dependent upon any harmful substance, we become open to Satan's influence. Small indiscretions and habits not consistent with the gospel of Jesus Christ can become great chains that bind us. "[Satan] leadeth them with a flaxen cord, until he bindeth them with his strong cords forever," the scriptures tell us. (2 Nephi 26:22) Small behaviors can ultimately lead to greater behaviors that entrap and enslave.

Not Controlling Our Thoughts

One man could pinpoint a time in his life when he became vulnerable to outside enticements because he felt as if he had never learned to control his thoughts adequately. Any time a man or woman lets his or her mind wander from a partner, he or she becomes vulnerable to Satan and his temptations. Spencer W. Kimball warns against any "married people" who "permit their eyes to wander and their hearts to become vagrant," who "have desire for someone other than the wife or the husband." *(The Miracle of Forgiveness*, p. 250) This lack of control over thoughts is often a precursor to other sins that can ultimately lead to infidelity. Thoughts in turn produce desires and subsequently our actions.

Abinadi warned King Noah and his priests, "Remember that he that persists in his own carnal nature, and goes on in the ways of sin and rebellion against God, remaineth in his fallen state and the devil hath all power over him." (Mosiah 16:5) Controlling our thoughts is the first step to overcoming our carnal natures.

Pornography

More than one person has traced his or her sexual immorality back to an exposure and subsequent addiction to pornography. In *The Worth of a Soul,* Steven A. Cramer described his addiction to pornography this way:

> I know that our Church leaders are totally correct when they warn that pornography is just as addictive and destructive as drugs and alcohol. Feeding upon its own awful lust, the viewing of pornography creates an ever-growing hunger for more and more filth. Like a runaway cancer, it is never satisfied but demands more and more until the victim can scarcely think of anything else. (p. 8)

His book describes the process of how his addiction to pornography led him to an affair. The affair and the resulting heartache took him, his wife and family much time, effort and faith to overcome.

Lack of Sufficient Consequence for Earlier Transgression

One man, who had been a bishop for several years and had dealt with serious transgressions during the time of his calling, noticed a common thread throughout the histories of many who had participated in the sin of sexual immorality. Many times these people had struggled with indiscretions in their youth but had not been sufficiently punished for those indiscretions. He described it as a "slap on the hand" for something he considered serious transgression, transgression which he felt probably should have been handled with harsher discipline. The counsel Elder Richard G. Scott once gave to parents might apply here. He said, "Don't make the mistake of purposefully intervening to soften or eliminate the natural consequences of your child's deliberate decisions to violate the commandments. Such acts reinforce false principles, *open the door for more serious sin*, and lessen the likelihood of repentance." (*Ensign*, May 1993, italics added)

"They Did Labor Diligently, Exhorting With All Long-Suffering the People to Diligence" (Jarom 1:11)

Since it is the small and simple things that make us open to transgression, it is the small and simple things that help make us resistant to it. Just as we must avoid the simple acts that lead us downward, we must adopt the simple behaviors that keep us strong and resistant to temptation and the whisperings of Satan. Prophets and apostles exhort us to daily diligence, keeping us "continually watchful unto prayer" (Moroni 6:4) because they know the powerful barrier to sin the simple act of prayer is. Consistent scripture reading, attendance at church meetings and consistent temple attendance can help us avoid the imbalances that may lead to temptation. As Alma counseled his son Helaman, "Do not let us be slothful because of the easiness of the way. ...The way is prepared, and if we will look we may live forever." (Alma 37:46)

5

"Satan Had Gotten Great Hold Upon the Hearts of the People" (Alma 8:9)

Whenever Satan can sense anything amiss in our lives, he will use all the means and tactics he can to lead us into temptation, sin and subsequent bondage to him. Where the sin of infidelity is involved, Satan's works are often manifested in one of two ways. In the first instance, Satan may simultaneously lead two people through the process of infidelity together. They're both essentially learning to sin as they buy into Satan's whisperings, lies and deceit. They become each other's confidants and allies as they move together toward inappropriate behavior.

On the other hand, Satan will often use someone already well-versed and practiced in sin as a tool to bring those who are vulnerable down to the depths of sin. They are truly "false prophets, who come to you in sheep's clothing, but inwardly they are ravening wolves" (3 Nephi 14:15) — in other words, they are people who lie in wait to deceive and destroy. Through flattery and lying words, these people often entice away those who have become susceptible. These people become instruments of Satan and are essentially perpetrators of sin. Knowingly or unknowingly, they perpetuate evil and darkness through their words and their actions. Alma the Younger is an example of someone who was once a perpetrator of sin. He became a wicked and idolatrous man. The scriptures tell us:

He was a man of many words, and did speak much flattery to the people; therefore *he led many of the people to do after the manner of his iniquities.*

And he became a great hinderment to the prosperity of the church of God; stealing away the hearts of the people...giving a chance for the enemy of God to exercise his power over them. (Mosiah 27:8-9, italics added)

Many perpetrators truly steal away the hearts of the people and lead them into sin. As an example, one man was known to have several affairs with different women, including two who were within the same ward boundaries as he was. One of these affairs resulted in the breakup of that woman's family and marriage. As another example, there was a woman who had several affairs in the course of a few years. She had married in the temple but broke apart her first marriage and then her second due to her infidelity. She essentially became practiced and hardened in the ways of sin. She then set her sights on one wealthy man who had been married in the temple and had been with his wife for over thirty-five years, a man who had held many weighty callings at both the ward and stake levels.

This woman began a slow, meticulous process of seduction. She began calling this man on the phone, claiming she was being stalked by someone but did not want to tell her own family "because her father would worry too much about her." She often called this man on the phone, asking for his help and preying upon his instinctive desires to comfort and protect her. Her calls continued throughout several months as she sought opportunities to see him. Through time and through her efforts, she was able to ultimately convince this man that he was not happy in his marriage, that he was the only man for her and that she was the only one who appreciated him adequately. She claimed she loved him and that they should be together and share this wonderful association they had. She somehow convinced this man that the Lord had brought about and sanctioned their relationship and that they were "meant for each other." Thus began an affair which led to living together outside the bonds of marriage despite their knowledge of the gospel and participation in previous temple ordinances. The affair resulted in the breakup of this man's eternal family.

Elder Richard G. Scott has warned those who sin, "None of your partners in error will help you onto the upward path. They think only of themselves. [See D& C 10:25] You know the result of following their path—unhappiness, failure, disappointment, and greater fear. They don't love you. They want to use you. Don't listen to them." (*Ensign*, May 1990) People such as this are truly wolves who lie in wait to destroy the flock. They are people who are instruments in Satan's hands to continue the work of destruction among choice sons and daughters of God. Through lies and deceit, they perpetuate evil and work tirelessly to bring others into the bondage of sin.

6

The Downward Cycle That Leads to Infidelity

Satan many times begins the process of infidelity very subtly. As two people form an association where they look for emotional support or understanding from someone besides a spouse, they become open to Satan's promptings and influence. As mentioned before, these promptings might be thoughts put in their minds by Satan or actual words and ideas spoken by a "perpetrator," a person who leads another down the path of transgression. This emotional attachment becomes the groundwork Satan must have to further the downward cycle of infidelity.

Satan then begins the initial stages of infidelity by convincing these people that all is not well within their homes or in their marriages—that in fact, their marriages never have been healthy or fulfilling. To reinforce this, he reminds them of every bad thing that has ever transpired with their spouses— every fight, argument or disagreement, every misunderstanding, hardship or trial. He hasn't forgotten these and he makes sure they now remember them and that they come to the forefront of their minds constantly. Next, Satan embellishes these past hurts and hardships to make them seem as if they have encompassed the whole of their married lives. Their marriages have been plagued with problems from the beginning, he tells them, even during their engagement and previous association. In essence, the adversary helps them re-write the history of their pasts, filling it with all of this contention, darkness, fighting, hardship, unhappiness and lack of fulfillment.

Straying spouses soon begin to view their spouses in this negative light—as contentious and vengeful, as emotionally unhealthy and manipulative, as unkind, uncaring and neglectful. Straying spouses come to believe that their partners have never given them the time, attention or love they needed or deserved. They convince themselves that their spouses have always been selfish, self-centered or not emotionally mature enough to maintain a healthy relationship needed for a marriage. *Their spouses are not spouses in the true sense of the word,* they might conclude, *so in essence, they never really did have a marriage, did they? Could the relationship they have now even be called a marriage?*

Straying spouse convince themselves that they've always been dissatisfied, unhappy and unfulfilled. Even though they've shared intimacy and good times with their current spouses, they become convinced that any good feelings that went along with these experiences were the result of disillusioned thinking. In fact, now that they have time to view their marriages in a true light, they come to believe their decisions to marry were pressured, coerced or made because their spouses carefully hid all the negative personality traits they had.

Once straying parties reach this avenue of thinking, often Satan prods them into subtle or open attacks against their spouses—what might be termed "spouse bashing"—in an attempt to wound, hurt or destroy them. These attacks are varied but they are usually attacks on a spouse's character, behaviors, spirituality or emotional health. They might even be attacks on physical appearance. Sometimes these attacks are centered on past decisions or choices the spouse has made and the supposed negative ramifications of them. Selfishness, hypocrisy, the inability to love appropriately and the inability to show true concern are often condemned.

These attacks are always somehow justified. The sinning parties say to themselves, "This is righteous indignation, isn't it? I'm fighting what's evil and destructive, am I not? I'm fighting what's held me down for years. I'm fighting unhappiness and misery because I won't put up with this anymore. I'm finally going to assert myself and get out of this bondage. I'm fighting a marriage plagued with problems. It's something I should have done long ago."

Many times the spouses of straying parties sense the conflict and tension in their marriages and begin fighting back as they try to work on the problems that have arisen between them. This only adds fuel to a straying partner's fire. As they witness their spouses' behavior, they think, *Here's proof of what I believe. See how contentious this person is, how angry and vengeful, how unloving and unkind? Now I see clearly what's happened to me all these years. Here's proof.* In essence, the spouse is blamed for all current and past problems in this person's life and because of this, the straying spouse comes to feel he or she is justified in looking outward for love and understanding.

This type of thinking becomes the basis for justifying any relationship that has begun outside of a marriage. In this relationship, sinning parties are led to believe that they have finally found true love—someone who will praise, adore and flatter them and someone who will complement and love them deeply. They feel they've finally discovered someone who truly understands all the pains and heartaches they've experienced through the years. They believe they deserve the attention they have been starved for, attention they've never had before. They believe that in this outside relationship, they will no longer have any of the problems or stresses that have fettered their current lives and marriages. They are truly happy and fulfilled—and spiritually whole, they conclude—being with this other person who cares so much about them.

As thinking like this grows and intensifies, it opens up straying parties to behaviors they might not have ever imagined themselves participating in before, particularly physical intimacy outside the bonds of marriage. This intimacy may begin with simple hugs or holding hands and then move on toward something more, maybe an occasional kiss "just to show my appreciation and gratitude for your kindness and thoughtful caring of me." Intimacy can grow from kissing to other behaviors beyond that or the contact may remain at the more simple forms of affection, affection someone may easily justify as acceptable.

Some people justify errant behavior on the grounds that they never did share any deep physical contact with this other person other than maybe hugs, holding hands or a few brief kisses. Still, these people go through the same cycles emotionally as those who do participate in the more serious sin of adultery. The justification of these lesser behaviors and participation therein could be considered the "adultery in their hearts" the Lord warns us about in the scriptures. (D&C 63:16)

As straying parties become involved in physical or emotional intimacy, soon there arises a distinct emotional change in them. They become emotionally distanced from their current partners. The distance may expand to the point where there is a complete lack of concern, caring or compassion for their current spouses. Sometimes, however, an odd behavior accompanies this portion of the cycle of infidelity that I've come to compare to an experience in my childhood.

The Stolen Lunch Money

During my grade school years, we lived far enough away from the elementary school that we had to ride the bus to get there. Each morning my brothers and sisters and I would walk to the bus stop and then place all of our books and possessions on the ground and go off to play with the other children. On one particular Monday, I remember carefully placing my books down and then setting my lunch money on top of them. I hurried and went off to play with some of the other children, not giving a second thought to my money lying out in the open.

When I returned to the bus line, however, I was astounded to see that someone had taken my lunch money. I couldn't believe it. I panicked. I was near tears wondering what my teacher would say and if I would be able to eat lunch that day. One little girl, Jane, saw my desperation and came to my side to comfort and console me. Jane spoke kind words to me and allowed me to go ahead of her in line "because you lost your money." She whispered to her brother, who was nearby, "Be nice to her because someone stole her lunch money." I felt drawn to her as I saw her comfort and concern for me.

Later on that day, as we were preparing for the bus ride home from school, Jane's cousin came up to me. "I know who took your money," she said as she handed the money back to me. "It was Jane. I found the money in her pocket." I was shocked. Here the girl who'd expressed love and concern for me had been the one to take my lunch money. She had been the one to cause my grief and then she'd played upon those feelings with her show of supposed concern and love. She had mocked me by pretending to care about me during this experience.

I've often thought about Jane's behavior. Why did Jane act that particular way toward me, showing compassion and concern when she knew full well she had been the one who had caused my hurt? Was she truly sorry for the pain she caused? Was she compassionate about the desperation I'd felt or was she taunting me with the inward knowledge that she'd gotten away with something? What kind of game was she playing? I don't know and I'm not sure I'll ever know. There is a behavior, however, that often goes along with the cycle of infidelity that brings about the same types of questions.

Often when a person begins to sin with another person and still feels guilt for his or her actions, sometimes that person will compensate for that guilt by lavishing a spouse, for a time, with gifts, kind words, gestures of love, attention and praise. Sometimes this false showing of love and concern may be directed toward others besides the spouse. For example, often a straying party will lavish attention, time and even money on the children of the person he or she is seeing. One woman who had become interested in a married man began spending time with some of his children, even during periods when the man was not around. The children, unaware of this woman's intent, talked often of her and began seeking out her association.

Other times, this false showing of love may be directed toward the other's spouse. In one instance, a woman who had become romantically interested in her neighbor began befriending that man's wife and spending a great deal of time with her. This was done without this woman's knowledge of what was happening between this neighbor and her husband.

"Suffer None of These Things to Enter into Your Heart" (3 Nephi 12:29)

As it says in the scriptures:

> Behold, it is written by them of old time, that thou shalt not commit adultery;

But I say unto you, that whosoever looketh
on a woman, to lust after her, hath committed
adultery already in his heart.

Behold, I give unto you a commandment,
that ye suffer none of these things to enter into your
heart;

For it is better that ye should deny yourselves
of these things, wherein ye will take up your cross,
than that ye should be cast into hell. (3 Nephi 12:27-30)

Many times an outside relationship, whether or not it
includes physical intimacy, is powerfully enticing in terms of
the emotional fulfillment one believes he or she can receive
from it. The Lord knows of this powerful enticement. More
importantly, He knows the dangers of the path this may lead
one into and that seeking temporary pleasures and gratification
may ultimately destroy eternal happiness. That is why He
reminds us forcefully that it is better "to take up your cross"
than to be "cast into hell." (3 Nephi 12:30)

All marriages, at one time or another, have been plagued
with difficulties. As one man teaching an institute class stated,
"In all marriages there would be adequate grounds for divorce.
That is because we are dealing with two imperfect people." This
does not mean we should leave someone solely because we feel
unfulfilled, unloved or misunderstood. Rather, as Moroni
reminds us, we must have "charity." (Moroni 7:44)

And charity suffereth long, and is kind, and
envieth not, and is not puffed up, *seeketh not her
own,* is not easily provoked, thinketh no evil, and
rejoiceth not in iniquity but rejoiceth in the truth,
beareth all things, believeth all things, hopeth all
things, endureth all things. ...Charity never faileth.

...But charity is the pure love of Christ, and
it endureth forever.

...Wherefore, my beloved brethren, pray

unto the Father with all the energy of thy heart, that ye may be filled with this love, which he hath bestowed upon all who are true followers of his Son, Jesus Christ. (Moroni 7:45-48)

Charity becomes the answer to those who are seeking something outside a marriage relationship for fulfillment. The gift of charity brings true peace and lasting happiness. Infidelity in any form will never be the answer but only brings about further sorrow and greater heartache.

7

"I Could Write a Book on True Love"

One of the deepest ironies that lies in an adulterous relationship is the fact that these people feel like they have found the deepest, most sacred, fulfilling, overpowering and pure love they could ever expect to find. They are literally consumed by love for this other person. One man who was involved in an adulterous relationship told a friend once, "I could write a book on true love." Another woman, who had married a man with whom she had an affair, told her sister-in-law, "I love him so much I never want to be away from him. I always want to be by his side. There's so much peace in our home from the love we share."

These people somehow come to believe that the love they have is so pure and undefiled that it will break all bounds that might stop it. For instance, if the two of them have been previously sealed to others, they believe those sealings will be easily canceled because of this other love—the love that was meant to be and the love certainly ordained and sanctioned by the Lord. Even if they know their relationship started inappropriately, they often adopt an attitude of, "If it so be that we are guilty, God will beat us with a few stripes, and at last we shall be saved in the kingdom of God." (2 Nephi 28:8) In other words, they might be punished a little for their indiscretions, but this wonderful relationship will never be taken away from them due to its basis. The Lord has told us, however, that "if it be not built upon my gospel, and is built upon the works of men, or upon the works of the devil, verily I say unto you they have joy in their works for a season, and by and by the end cometh." (3 Nephi 27:11) This kind of love is not everlasting love, the charity the Lord speaks about. It is a love based on selfishness and lust. Although they have "joy in their works for a season...by and by the end cometh" unless there is complete repentance. (Moroni 7:46)

"Thou Art Possessed With a Lying Spirit" (Alma 30:42)

Many who have begun to participate in behaviors that lead to infidelity go through a period of time when they try to hide their sins and indiscretions from their current partners and everyone around them. They might continue to try to keep their sins secret up until the point their indiscretions are discovered by an outside party. In order to hide like this, Satan usually helps them form a careful, systematic pattern of lies. For some, they might claim there are increasing demands at work that may take them out of town or keep them away into the late hours of the night. For others, they might pretend to be spending "needed time alone" or "needed time away from the family," especially if they are trying to escape the "problems we always have at home" and the misery their spouses cause them.

Other excuses are made for time away, as well. One woman claimed the time she spent from home during her affair was time spent with a therapist as she worked on some of her marital and emotional problems. Other excuses and lies come about but lies are always a part of the behavior of anyone involved in infidelity.

Usually these people become deeply skilled at lying. Sometimes, like Korihor in the *Book of Mormon*, they repeat these lies and deceptions for so long they come to "verily [believe] that they [are] true." (Alma 30:53) These lies become embedded in the thinking patterns they adopt and no one can convince them of past realities or the truth. When they hear the truth, they are often angry and offended for the "guilty taketh the truth to be hard, for it cutteth them to the very center." (1 Nephi 16:2)

A hostile reaction to the truth usually includes the alienation of the one who has spoken, a reaction which comes about because sinning parties are not "willing to hearken to the truth, and give heed unto it." (1 Nephi 16:3) They have become so entrenched in transgression and sin that they, at this point, have no desire to change. Avoiding and fighting the truth like this through lying helps them rationalize their sinful behaviors so they can continue in them.

"I, the Lord, Am Not to Be Mocked" (D&C 63:58)

Anyone who "has set at naught the counsels of God, and has broken the most sacred promises which were made before God" (D&C 3:13) by being involved in infidelity surely mocks the Lord through his or her actions. These people have truly broken some of the most sacred covenants which were made under heaven, especially if they participated in a temple sealing or were baptized members of the Lord's Church.

A friend of mine had an interesting experience with a woman she met at a health spa. She came to find out that this woman was a member of the Church but had been having an affair with another man for quite some time. This woman almost seemed to glory in her wickedness. She told my friend, "All you have to do is what you've always done and no one knows that you're having an affair. Go to church, attend your meetings, and do all the same things you used to do and no one even suspects."

My friend was not only appalled but surprised by this seemingly callous attitude toward sin. As she drove away from the spa thinking about this situation, the Lord whispered into her mind, "I, the Lord, will not be mocked." Though this woman's sins were "done in secret," (Moses 5:30) these things were not "hid from the Lord" (Moses 5:39) and the Lord would not be mocked in these things.

The Lord warns adulterers and adulteresses that they should "beware and repent speedily, lest judgment shall come upon them as a snare, and their folly shall be made manifest, and their works shall follow them in the eyes of the people." (D&C 63:15) Though works of darkness might be temporarily hidden, they will be brought to light. As Richard G. Scott once stated:

> Do not take comfort in the fact that your transgressions are not known by others. That is like an ostrich with his head buried in the sand. He sees only darkness and feels comfortably hidden. In reality he is ridiculously conspicuous. Likewise our every act is seen by our Father in Heaven and His Beloved Son. They know everything about us.
>
> Excusing transgression with a cover-up may appear to fix the problem but it does not. *The tempter is intent on making public your most embarrassing acts at the most harmful time.* (*Ensign*, May 1995, italics added)

As often happens, though these people try to hide their sins, "the show of their countenance doth witness against them," (2 Nephi 13:9) an outward indication that they are caught in the web of transgression. Countenances often show the darkness that has come about because of evil choices. For example, one woman, looking back on her experiences with a sister-in-law who had an affair, related an experience she'd had before she came to realize this woman had been committing adultery. They had agreed to meet for lunch at a specific time and place and this woman happened to look up when her sister-in-law entered the restaurant. For a moment, she felt startled at what she saw. "I had always thought she was beautiful, but when I looked at her on this day, there was this darkness about her, almost as if she looked sick. I studied her for awhile, trying to understand what it was—why it was that she looked so different." She later came to find out this change of appearance had come about from her participation in adultery.

The Lord often gives others ways and means of helping them discover "secret works of darkness." (2 Nephi 10:15) Sometimes transgressors are caught in their behaviors or sometimes others are given knowledge through the Spirit that something is going on. One woman, through several impressions, came to realize that her daughter was involved in sexual immorality. This daughter came to realize that even if she thought her works were secret, the Lord could make them known unto her mother. She therefore checked herself in these behaviors and began the road to repentance.

The best scenario for transgressors, obviously, is that their works are brought to light through confessions that are not forced—in other words, when they confess on their own volition and not because they are "compelled to be humble" (Alma 32:14) because they have been found out. Usually progress toward repentance is more swift and certain with this type of attitude, an attitude where transgressors realize the seriousness of their sins and desire to find the path to wholeness.

Weak in the Space of Not Many Years

Once a person has begun to sin or become established in a pattern of continuing sin and does not seek repentance, this can, as Elder Stephen D. Nadauld once explained, make people "become *weak*, because of their transgression, *in the space of not many years* [Hel. 4:27]. Whether it be individuals or a whole society, it is possible that decay from within can wreak havoc in a relatively short time." (*Ensign*, July 1996)

Often those who have known and loved straying parties who become involved in transgression are astounded at the level and depth of sin these people reach in a seemingly short time, especially if they have been unaware of the transgression. Many straying parties seem to undergo personality changes. They may become contentious, angry, vicious and easily offended whereas they might have been good-natured and easygoing before. They may begin to lie and tell falsehood so frequently and so often that one does not know when to believe anything they say anymore.

Others move on to behaviors and sins that seem shocking to those who have known them previously—sins such as homosexuality, multiple affairs, participation in prostitution, sexual abuse, or other serious forms of transgression. Many lose their testimonies, their faith in God, and their desire to attend church. Sometimes they will become antagonistic toward the Church and its members and express much anger and resentment toward God and His Son for trials or anguish that have come about in their lives. Many transgressors may become perpetrators of sin, leading others down the paths they have chosen. Whatever happens may happen quickly, leaving those on the outside looking on in consternation at the rapid spiritual decline of those they are concerned about. Darkness and evil seem to snowball and fill their lives in ever-increasing amounts unless stopped by true repentance.

The Spouse is Always the Last to Know

The saying that "the spouse is always the last to know" often holds truth in dealing with transgressors. Often the closer one is to the situation of infidelity, the longer it may take for that person to actually become aware of, understand and admit to the true extent of what is happening or what has happened to a straying loved one. This statement of being "the last to know" not only seems true for a partner who has been betrayed but also for family members or other associates close to the situation.

Two different scenarios might hold some weight in dealing with this enigma. The first might be called "The Boiling Frog Syndrome." Supposedly, if you put a frog into a pot of hot water, it will quickly jump out of it. Conversely, however, if you slowly warm the water by degrees, the frog will stay in the water until the water gets so hot, the temperature kills it. "The change [is] so gradual, almost imperceptible, that the frogs [accommodate] themselves to their new environment—until it [is] too late," President James E. Faust stated. (*Ensign*, April 1996)

So it might be with one living with a transgressor. The changes in a transgressor's life sometimes occur so subtly and slowly a person close to the situation might not see the changes as clearly. Someone on the outside, who may not have such immediate and constant contact, might be able to discern the changes accompanying sin more easily.

Another scenario that might hold some truth is the fact that often a transgressor can deceive more readily someone they know very well. They know the thought patterns, personality traits, weaknesses and vulnerabilities of their partners, their families and close associates. Knowing these traits, they can thus deceive in accordance to what they know. Kristine's husband, for example, would often go off on long, unexplained trips to visit his "friends" in another city. As he distanced himself more and more from his wife, his wife's family—who did not live near them at the time—quickly began to suspect his increasingly odd behaviors might be linked to infidelity. He, however, would excuse his absences by saying he needed time away to sort things out, that his wife "had never made him happy," that "she didn't care about him" and that "she needed to change" before he could continue in their relationship.

Kristine worked relentlessly during this time, agreeing to try to do those things he claimed she needed to do in order for him to become happy and fulfilled. She felt increasing surprise and despair as he continued to leave their home despite her sincere efforts to overcome their problems. Kristine finally questioned her husband directly about his behavior. She questioned him openly if he happened to be involved in infidelity. He gave her a resounding "No!" Because he knew her so well, he told her other fabrications about his odd behavior, fabrications that she accepted. It wasn't until some time later, after several failed attempts to re-establish their relationship, that Kristine came to say, "I think my husband might be seeing someone else." She later discovered that he had been seeing another woman for over a year and a half of their marriage and had fathered another child during that time.

"How is it Ye Have Forgotten?" (1 Nephi 7:10)

When the works of darkness of one participating in infidelity are brought into the light, one who loves these sinning parties might feel like asking, as Nephi did of his wayward brothers Laman and Lemuel, "How is it ye have forgotten...?" (1 Nephi 7:10)

•How is it you have forgotten that you had a testimony of the Lord, Jesus Christ, and the truthfulness of His ways?

•How is it you've forgotten you've gone on a mission or made sacred covenants in the temple?

•How is it you've forgotten that for the greater part of your life you've tried to keep the commandments of the Lord?

•How is it you've forgotten that you've had deep spiritual experiences that you cherished?

•How is it that you've forgotten you once loved your current spouse and you had many good experiences and much happiness together?

•How is it you've forgotten that you are participating in sins and transgression you warned your children against?

Questions similar to these might arise as someone struggles with the difficulty of seeing those lost in sin. Resultant sorrow might be very similar to Nephi's sorrow for his brothers when he said, "Behold, my soul is rent with anguish because of you, and my heart is pained," (1 Nephi 17:47) or his father's sorrow when he said to Laman and Lemuel, "My heart hath been weighed down with sorrow from time to time, for I have feared, lest for the hardness of your hearts the Lord your God should come out in the fulness of his wrath upon you, that ye be cut off and destroyed forever." (2 Nephi 1:17)

When a straying party has reached a point when he or she is truly bound by the chains of infidelity, those who love that person may mourn even as Enoch mourned over the wickedness of the children of men. "Enoch...looked upon their wickedness, and their misery, and wept and stretched forth his arms, and his heart swelled wide as eternity; and his bowels yearned; and all eternity shook." (Moses 7:41) This may be an adequate description of the pain and anguish many experience because of the consequences of infidelity. The only source of comfort and peace for this pain will come through Jesus Christ, who understands the depths of sin and the resulting sorrow that comes from it.

8

"I Did Pour Out My Soul Unto God For Them" (Enos 1:9)

Once someone becomes entrenched in transgression and does not desire to change, often the love, caring, compassion and faith of those on the outside who know that person can become instrumental in moving him or her toward an acknowledgment of sins and from there toward repentance. Satan knows this. He knows that others' faith and prayers can have a powerful effect on the healing process of a transgressor, that through others' faith the Lord can work miracles in their lives. (Ether 12:12) He also knows, as Richard G. Scott once stated, that, "Love is a potent healer. Realizing that, Satan would separate [a transgressor] from the power of the love of God, kindred, and friends that want to help." (*Ensign*, May 1994)

It is no wonder that Satan tries to convince those involved in sin to hide their transgressions for as long as possible so people who might want to help have no idea what is going on. It is no wonder that Satan, through his promptings and influence, tries to get transgressors alienated from all those who love and might try to help them—particularly family members, friends, close associates and priesthood leaders. He often tries to turn transgressors against those who would be the most beneficial in terms of helping them with spiritual healing.

"They Were Angry Because They Had Testified So Plainly Against Their Wickedness" (Alma 14:3)

Transgressors often become angry at the words of truth spoken by those who are trying to help. Often they turn against others who might try to call them to repentance. "If you really loved and cared about me," they might say, "then you wouldn't question what I'm feeling or the decisions I'm making. You would understand how awful and destructive my marriage has been, how rotten my spouse is and how much hurt my spouse has caused me. You wouldn't tell me it's wrong to leave my current spouse for this person the Lord has brought into my life. Besides, you were never there in the past. You never saw what happened in my marriage. How come you try to tell me what to do when you don't even know me, when you don't understand me or attempt to understand what I've been through?"

Many transgressors become easily offended at innocent remarks of family members or close associates and they often misconstrue entirely the meaning of words or gestures of love and compassion from them. Because of these supposed offenses, transgressors justify withdrawing themselves from loved ones' association and influence. Often, too, offense is taken from the words and actions of priesthood leaders who have a calling to help, warn and discipline them. Satan will spend much of his time trying to cut off transgressors from the love and concern of those who might help them find their way back to the Savior. Then he can continue on with the work of destruction he has effectively begun.

"Satan Seeketh to Destroy" (D&C 132:57)

Leslie noticed an interesting occurrence that happened in her family as the transgressions of one of her sisters came to light. When it became known among the parents and each of the brothers and sisters in her family that her sister had been involved in an adulterous relationship, there seemed to be an onslaught of contention and bickering in each of their respective marriages, including that of the parents. There were petty disagreements and contention between each of the couples who had a concern for this sister.

Leslie marveled at this occurrence. She came to believe that Satan had tried to sidetrack them all from offering their help, love and prayers of concern for this sister by getting them all involved in problems of their own. Once Leslie noticed this happening, she prayed that she and the rest of her family would be safeguarded from the influences of Satan and his forces so that they could in turn help their sister through their efforts and prayers. Leslie literally felt an outpouring of the Spirit and felt attendant spirits from the other side of the veil give help, comfort and assistance. She could see a noticeable difference in their lives after these prayers seeking protection.

Tiffany had been putting forth effort and time in helping one of her struggling brothers. She spent a great deal of time and energy in this brother's behalf only to find out that her motives, efforts and attempts to help were attacked and criticized by other family members. She became troubled and tearful, wondering if her efforts had been futile and wondering if she'd done more harm than good. In trying to garner the strength to deal with these issues, she asked for a priesthood blessing. "The adversary is trying to weaken your influence [with your brother] by influencing others," she was told. "Remember that the Lord is stronger. Continue prayer and scripture study, and the Lord will make you stronger and more capable of influence." Tiffany knew, after this experience, that whenever Satan could not work on her directly, he would try to use others to stop her righteous efforts. She came to realize, however, that the Lord would expand and magnify her actions so that she, despite the adversary's attempts to stop her, could truly end up being an instrument for good—with the continued help of the Lord. Those who seek to be a force of righteousness in the lives of transgressors need to seek the same protective blessings from the Lord to help them combat the dark forces that Satan inevitably garners whenever there has been infidelity in any form.

9

Early Priesthood Intervention

The earlier the transgressions of a sinner are known by those who want to help and counsel that person, the better chance for recovery and the quicker may be the return to wholeness. One woman who counseled with her stake president after he had dealt with hundreds of cases of infidelity, besides her own husband's, was told by him, "In my experience, most often success with a transgressor depends on when it is that priesthood leaders become involved. The most success in turning a transgressor around and saving a marriage has come from early priesthood intervention." In other words, the sooner the transgressions had become known to those holding the priesthood who could counsel and direct these transgressors, the more likely they would remain with their current spouses and begin the repentance process. Obviously this is not true for everyone but as a general rule it helps to know that the sooner a transgressor becomes accountable for his or her actions, the better it is in terms of the chances for spiritual healing and recovery.

Sympathy

We must be extremely careful in our offerings of sympathy and understanding toward those involved in transgression. As Boyd K. Packer once said, "If we, out of sympathy, should approve unworthy conduct, it might give present comfort to someone, but would not ultimately contribute to their happiness." (*Ensign*, Nov. 1995) One can be loving and tolerant of the sinner without being tolerant of the sin.

One man, who was trying to give strength and support to someone he knew who was involved in sin, began to believe the lies and the stories this person told to justify sinful behaviors. Soon he became this person's ally and turned against others who were trying to help, saying, "— — is right. We don't really know what happened in this marriage. We have no right to judge or intervene. We should all just be supporting and loving."

Not long after these declarations, after this man had been able to have some time away from the situation, he realized what he had done—that he had been caught up in this person's deception. He realized his behavior might have contributed to the fact that this person still felt justified in continuing on with the choices that were being made instead of trying to repent. Once this man no longer continued supporting this person verbally in this way, the sinning party soon turned against him, saying he no longer understood and that he was no longer helpful. The sinning party became angry and bitter toward him and would no longer listen to anything he had to say.

"It's Your Job to Love Me Unconditionally"

The only times I have ever heard people make requests for someone to love them and accept them unconditionally, without "judging" them, have been times when transgressors or those supporting them are asking for support for their choices and decisions, support that they believe should be given without questioning their motives, decisions or behaviors. Laman and Lemuel in their wickedness murmur against their father saying that they "know that the people who were in the land of Jerusalem were a righteous people...and *our father hath judged them.*" (1 Nephi 17:22, italics added) When the wicked King Noah heard the words of Abinadi, he questioned, "Who is Abinadi, that I and my people should be *judged* of him?" (Mosiah 11:27, italics added) As another example, one daughter felt impressed by the Lord, through her scripture reading and priesthood blessings, to warn her father about the spiritual consequences of his affair. She attempted many times, both verbally and in writing, to tell him that his chosen decisions were wrong, that they went against everything he had previously stood for and that they went against everything he had taught her to avoid. She tried to help him see the pain and anguish he had caused not only his wife but his children—her brothers and sisters—as well.

During one heated conversation, the father said to her, "It isn't your job to judge me. The Lord tells us we should never judge, to leave it alone with Him. It is your job to love me unconditionally. That is the only thing you should be doing, the only thing required of you. Otherwise, get out of my life and leave me alone." What he was saying, in essence, was that he wanted her to let him go on in the ways of sin and rebellion without trying to stop him. He wanted to move forward with what he was doing with no one calling him to repentance or telling him of the spiritual ramifications of his actions.

The Lord tells us not to judge others but He also asks us to "judge righteously" so that we may discern the ways of truth and avoid the pitfalls of sin. (Alma 41:14) Trying to help and warn others of the destructive choices of infidelity is not judging but an attempt to help and warn them, an attempt to help them find a better path—a voice of warning, in essence. The Lord tells us in the *Doctrine & Covenants* that we are "called to cry repentance unto this people." (D&C 18:14) Truly it is our duty and sacred obligation to warn those we love of the effects and consequences of infidelity. It is not judging but loving them that draws us to do this. It is only a concern for their eternal welfare that these efforts are given in their behalf.

Prayers of Faith

When a transgressor fights every effort on the part of others to help, often it is only through our prayers of faith that they might ultimately be helped. Karen told of a time when she often prayed for a friend who became involved in sexual transgression. At first, Karen felt like she could see many of the fruits of her prayers. Her friend's heart seemed to soften and she began attending church meetings regularly. She seemed happy and open to counsel.

Suddenly, however, these behaviors began to change. This straying party once again pulled back and withdrew from social interaction involving Karen. She stopped attending meetings and seemed to become more hardened and brusque in any interaction with people who desired to assist her. Karen suddenly felt like all of her prayers had been futile and that she was not even helping in any way. Why should she continue to try to put forth any efforts for this straying party?

The same thought crossed Karen's mind as she was about to put her friend's name on the temple prayer roll. *Why even do it?* she asked herself as she turned to walk away. *It doesn't help*. Immediately an answering thought from the Lord entered her mind. "You don't know what I can do," the Lord told her. She quickly turned around and put that person's name on the prayer roll. Karen came to understand that, although she saw no results from her efforts and prayers, the Lord was still able to work in areas of this straying party's life that she could not see or discern on her own. She also knew that despite what she saw on the outside, she should never stop her efforts of faith in her friend's behalf.

"It Shall Be Given You...What Ye Shall Say" (D&C 100:6)

The Lord has advised us, "Therefore, verily I say unto you, lift up your voices unto this people; speak the thoughts that I shall put into your hearts, and you shall not be confounded before men; For it shall be given you in the very hour, yea, in the very moment, what ye shall say." (D&C 100:5-6) This becomes true in our dealings with transgressors. Often it is given us what we shall say or do—even what we should pray for—in order to help those we love.

In the *Ensign*, a woman once told the story about her dealings with a wayward son who had been involved in serious transgression. Because this son had shunned all of her outward efforts of help, she put her time and strength into her prayers of faith for him. She prayed without ceasing, keeping his name on the prayer rolls of the temple and fasting for him every Sunday. Soon the Lord impressed into her mind that she should pray that someone her son respected would come into his life.

"The name of his former [Church] leader came to mind, a peace officer whom I saw soon after at stake conference," she wrote. "I told him about my son and the impression I'd had. He said without hesitation that he would go and see him." Later, she writes, "He...had gone where I could not go and be welcomed. My heart overflowed with gratitude.

"From that time on," she continued, "I felt powerful spiritual confidence infuse me. *I realized that my prayers were being heard and that deeply spiritual blessings could result if I would continue to be faithful and diligent in my efforts.*"

Her prayers continued. "One Monday morning as I prayed," she said, "I had a strong impression to ask Heavenly

Father to give my son a special dream, for it was only when he slept that he was still enough to listen. The specific words to say came gently to my mind. I was startled. I doubted that I had understood the impression correctly. Could I do such a thing? However, after receiving the same prompting two more times, I obeyed. As I knelt in prayer, I was moved to ask specifically that my son have a bright recollection of all his guilt and feel the burden of his sins, but also know immediately that the Savior loved him and wanted him back."

Not long after this prayer and experience, her son returned home, asking for forgiveness and telling his parents he wanted to go on a mission. When he spoke in stake conference some time later, he related the fact that he had returned to church activity because of a dream in which he had "a bright recollection of all my guilt. I felt the burden of my sins but knew immediately that the Savior loved me and wanted me back." What to pray for had been given to this woman and the results of her prayers were the return of her wayward son. (*Ensign*, April 1996, italics added)

Another woman who dealt with the transgressions of someone she loved felt led to pray that this person would be humbled through outside events of hardship because "for a man sometimes, if he is compelled to be humble, seeketh repentance; and now surely, whosoever repenteth shall find mercy." (Alma 32:13) This woman knew that because this person she loved had become so hardened and bound by iniquity, hardship in that person's life would be the only event that might bring this person down to the depths of humility. She knew that like Laman and Lemuel, "there was nothing save it were the power of God, which threatened them with destruction, could soften their hearts." (1 Nephi 18:20)

As she prayed for this, that the Lord would bring down

this person's transgressions "with sorrow upon [his] own [head]," (Enos 1:10) she came to understand through a priesthood blessing that the things she had prayed for "would come to pass," that "the time would come when they would be executed" and that the Lord's judgment would be upon "those who are wicked. They will feel the wrath of God," she was told. With this knowledge came the repeated assurance that the one she loved would repent. Knowing this, she could move on in faith, trusting that her faith and prayers would help influence the life of the one she loved.

Henry B. Eyring once gave further insight regarding praying for those lost in sin. He stated:

> Sometimes tragedy will soften a heart. But for some, tragedy is not enough. But there is one need even hardened and proud people cannot believe they can meet for themselves. They cannot lift the weight of sin from their own shoulders. And even the most hardened may at times feel the prick of conscience and thus the need for forgiveness from God. …Prayers are answered to those whose hearts are softened by that overwhelming feeling of the need for cleansing. (*Ensign*, Aug. 2009)

Alma's prayers for his wayward son, Alma the Younger, were instrumental in Alma the Younger feeling the weight of his sins. Alma the Younger explained, "For three days and for three nights was I racked, even with the pains of a damned soul. …I was harrowed up by the memory of my many sins." (Alma 36:16-17) Feeling this burdensome weight is what moved Alma the Younger toward repentance, cleansing and a life of service for the Savior.

After All You Can Do

Richard G. Scott once said:

> When the things you realistically can do to help a [transgressor] are done, leave the matter in the hands of the Lord and worry no more. Do not feel guilty because you cannot do more. Do not waste your energy on useless worry.
>
> ...In time, you will feel impressions and know how to give further help. You will find more peace and happiness, will not neglect others that need you, and will be able to give greater help because of that eternal perspective.
>
> Never give up on a loved one, never! (*Ensign*, May 1988)

As we labor with our might to help those we love who have been involved in infidelity, we must remember that, after all we can do—even if we do not see the desired course corrections in their lives—we must "trust [them] unto the Lord." (Alma 19:23) Often the Lord will give promised eternal blessings—anchors—that will sustain us enough to let go of those we love for awhile as they must go and suffer the consequences of their actions. We will not worry and fret so much about them and we will be able to function more effectively in our own lives, especially if we feel a spiritual reassurance that these people will one day return. As the prophet Jacob says in the *Book of Mormon*, "For because of faith and great anxiety, it truly had been made manifest unto us concerning our people, *what things should happen unto them.*" (Jacob 1:5, italics added)

One woman, Lana, was told in a priesthood blessing that the one she loved who was lost in sin would "one day cry bitter tears for all [this person] has done." She was also promised that she would have a spiritual manifestation to know when this had happened. From this knowledge, Lana felt assured that one day this straying loved one would realize the extent of the transgressions committed and then return to the Savior. With this knowledge, although she still had times of severe trial as she witnessed the continued path of darkness in this loved one's life, Lana was able to let go of the worry that had sidelined her own life. She soon functioned better and more effectively, felt more happiness and peace for longer periods of time and felt her trust in the Savior and His ways grow.

10

"I, the Lord, Will Contend With Zion and Chasten Her Until She Overcomes and is Clean Before Me" (D&C 90:36)

Anne had an interesting experience that helped her understand, through some of her own experiences, the feelings the Lord had for a transgressor she loved. This transgressor had participated in the deepest and most heart-wrenching transgression Anne had ever seen and yet seemed to show no remorse or regret for the hurt, anguish and pain caused by the betrayal. In fact, it seemed from superficial appearances that this transgressor suffered no effects from the serious sins committed. The transgressor acted happy and fulfilled and did not seem to deal with any of the repercussions one might suppose would come into the life of one who had strayed as deeply as this person had. This person had married the one who had been a partner in transgression and their lives seemed relatively unruffled and unchanged while those they had betrayed had been deeply hurt and scarred by their behavior, not only spiritually and emotionally but temporally, as well.

One day Anne had an experience that helped her to understand in a broader sense how the Lord viewed the situation. On this day, one of her children, a boy who seldom got into trouble, played "hooky" from kindergarten. Because of the persuasions of a friend, he purposefully missed the school bus and played in this friend's back yard until they were discovered some two hours later by this friend's mother. He was then sent home.

As Anne stood out on the front porch awaiting her son's return, she felt surprised to see her little son walking happily along, not feeling any remorse for his actions. He had a smile on his face that he did not hide from his mother. This mother suddenly felt the impact of what had happened. Here someone she loved, someone she loved deeply who she'd never had to punish harshly before, did not realize the seriousness of what he'd done or the possible negative consequences of his behaviors. He truly did not see anything wrong with the decision he'd made to stay home from school.

After her startled reaction to this seeming blatant unawareness of what he'd done, Anne immediately sent her son to his room so she could sort through her thoughts in knowing how to deal with him. She prayed as she struggled to know how to discipline her son effectively enough so that he would understand that his actions were serious and warranted punishment. Anne called her husband and together they decided on the punishment they felt was appropriate for him—the most severe punishment they had ever meted out to one of their children. They knew he needed to view his actions in the appropriate light and would only do this if his discipline was harsh enough to let him know he'd behaved badly.

Before she went to go to her son's bedroom to tell him what had been decided, Anne waited for awhile as she struggled with her feelings. She felt a great burden inside her. She loved this little boy with all her heart but she knew—for his safety and welfare—that he needed to feel the seriousness of what he'd done. As she felt the weight of how her little son would react as he suffered through his punishment, tears came to her eyes. His mistakes had not lessened her love for him in the least but it was that love that was a driving force behind the discipline that would be coming to him. The punishment came only as a deterrent to curb further behaviors in the future that could be detrimental to her son's safety and welfare.

As Anne thought over this, she felt an impression come into her mind from the Lord. "This is how I feel about ____ (the transgressor she'd been worried about)." This experience taught Anne a valuable lesson. She knew that the transgressor she'd been concerned about had behaved very similarly to her little son—that this person did not realize or feel any weight of the sins that had been committed. She also knew that the Lord must, through hardship and punishment, let this transgressor feel the weight of the sins and transgressions committed so it would be a deterrent to transgression in the future. More than anything, Anne felt the love of the Lord for this transgressor and the sadness that accompanied His having to chasten a beloved child in this way. She knew, however, that it was for this transgressor's welfare and benefit that the chastisement would be meted out.

Later, in dealing with her little son, Anne noticed a change in her son's attitude from "belligerent to humble." She felt this would be the change in this transgressor's life that would lead that person back to wholeness.

"Your Love Will Help More Than Anything You Can Say"

Often gestures of love are the only messages that get through to those who are lost in sin. Sometimes these gestures have the greatest impact on a transgressor's healing process. One mother struggled and prayed over what she should say to help her straying daughter return to the fold. What words of warning should she give this daughter? How often should she call this daughter to repentance? What was her responsibility in terms of making sure her daughter understood the consequences of her behavior and actions? She asked these questions over and over again, struggling with what the Lord required of her. In a priesthood blessing, she was told directly that her love for her daughter would help far more than anything she could say.

As this woman attempted to show this daughter her love, she saw this daughter's heart open up more to her influence. Her daughter began seeking her out, as well, for strength, guidance and support. This mother came to understand that her continued efforts to show love would ultimately be the most beneficial in her attempts to help her daughter return to wholeness.

Dealing with Anger for a Transgressor

Often those who have been affected by the transgressions of those they love feel great anger for these people. They struggle with the fact that they have caused so much pain and anguish in their lives and the lives of those around them. They might be angry at the way these transgressors have hurt their children, spouses and extended families and might have done it with seemingly little conscience.

One woman felt great anger for someone she knew who was lost in sin, anger that made it nearly impossible for her to speak or interact with that person. She had a priesthood blessing that helped her deal with the anger she felt. In that blessing, the Lord told her essentially that "anger is not a bad thing. Even the Lord gets angry. But the Lord uses anger constructively—to help and build people up and to help people repent." She was further told not to kill her feelings of anger but to try to understand their basis, that understanding and dealing effectively with them was necessary in our becoming as God is. After this blessing, this woman then pored over the scriptures, marking down passages dealing with the Lord's anger.

> I would let fall the sword of mine indignation in behalf of my people. (D&C 101:10)

> The indignation of the Lord is kindled against their abominations and all their wicked works. (D&C 97:24)

> I, the Lord, am angry with the wicked. (D&C 63:32)

This woman came to understand through the scriptures that the Lord indeed felt anger and indignation for sin but that He used this anger to help those He loved repent.

> Verily, thus saith the Lord unto you whom I love, and whom I love I also chasten that their sins may be forgiven, for with the chastisement I prepare a way for their deliverance in all things out of temptation, and I have loved you—
> Wherefore, ye must needs be chastened and stand rebuked before my face;
> For ye have sinned against me a very grievous sin. (D&C 95:1-3)

As this woman began to study the basis for her anger, she found out that some of her anger was based on disappointment—disappointment that someone she considered to be one of the children of light who had been taught in the "nurture and admonition of the Lord" (Enos 1:1) would allow Satan in to reap his destruction on this person and this person's family. She also came to understand that her anger was based partly on fear of the spiritual consequences of this loved one's actions. She also came to understand that what she truly desired, even more than to express her anger, was to see the day that this loved one would repent and turn once again to the Lord.

This woman felt grateful to know that the Lord was understanding of her anger and did not condemn her for it. As she came to understand this, the Lord helped her further by allowing her to see the basis for her anger and then move outward from there to using it constructively—helping the one she loved to repent through her efforts of love and through her prayers of faith.

How Can I Ever Learn to Forgive?

Often the abuses and the betrayal of those lost in sin are so great that the hurt and pain that arises seems impossible to overcome. Forgiveness seems unreachable and unobtainable. One woman expressed her feelings about her husband who had an affair and fathered another child during that time. He ultimately decided to give up this outside relationship and return to his family. "At first, I felt worse than hatred toward him. I felt apathy," this woman said. "I got to the point where I no longer even cared what happened to him or the choices he made. I felt no concern for him whatsoever."

She continues, "I can testify that the Lord can heal our relationships and help us learn to love again. He helped me come to the point where I am today when there was a time I never imagined it was possible. I can truly say that I've learned to love my husband again." This process of forgiveness, however, took her many years and much pain, heartache and inward searching to accomplish.

Often those who have been betrayed feel a great weight and burden knowing they need to forgive those who have hurt and harmed them because of infidelity. The Savior will truly take this burden of forgiveness upon Himself as He does all of the burdens we must carry. He will teach those who seek His will exactly what forgiveness is and what it entails for each specific experience, especially for those left alone and abandoned after a betrayal. It is a process of time, patience and effort—just as are all other steps toward righteousness.

Often people who have been injured think forgiveness means suddenly giving up all the negative emotions surrounding a betrayal and feeling immediate love and compassion for those who have hurt them. This is simply not true. The Lord will deal equitably with every situation of our lives until we will all see "eye to eye" and "confess before God that his judgments are just." (Mosiah 16:1) Forgiveness encompasses the ability to trust that the Lord will do this even with the losses, hurts and wrongs that arise from betrayals. Forgiveness is letting those burdens go to Him with the hope and faith that this will one day happen. The Lord has said, "By faith all things are fulfilled." (Ether 12:3) Certainly it is by faith that the Lord will lead feelings and emotions to the point where they need to be, especially in relation to forgiveness. Those who bear these heavy burdens can rest in the hope that the Savior accepts of their sacrifices and offerings even if they can only have the initial desire to *hope* to forgive some day. Like the seed that Alma speaks about, this desire can grow over time to become the tree that bears eternal fruit. "If ye will nourish the word, yea, nourish the tree as it beginneth to grow, by your faith with great diligence, and with patience, looking forward to the fruit thereof it shall take root; and behold it shall be a tree springing up unto everlasting life," the scriptures tell us. (Alma 32:41)

11

"The Word Which Healeth the Wounded Soul" (Jacob 2:8)

"Save for those few who defect to perdition after having known a fullness, there is no habit, no addiction, no rebellion, no transgression, no offense exempted from the promise of complete forgiveness," Boyd K. Packer once reminded us. (*Ensign*, Nov. 1995) Often those bound by the sin of infidelity lose sight of this anchor of hope. Often feelings of guilt and shame are so great that those who need help feel they will never be able to make their way back to the Savior.

"[Satan] wants you to believe you lack the capacity to help yourself," Richard G. Scott once said. "His strategy is to have you think you are not appreciated, loved or wanted so that you in despair will turn to self-criticism, and in the extreme to even despising yourself and feeling evil when you are not." (*Ensign*, May 1994) Steven A. Cramer describes the lies told him by Satan that led him to despair:

> The most vicious lie of all was that there are three kinds of people: celestial, terrestrial and telestial and that I would never become a celestial person. Over and over [Satan] asked when I was going to face up to this reality and quit torturing myself? Why was I making my life so miserable by trying to be more than I really was? Didn't the last twenty-eight years prove that I would be much more comfortable and, therefore, much happier in one of

the lower kingdoms? *(The Worth of A Soul, p. 17)*

Once someone is caught in the web of sin, "Lucifer will do all in his power to keep you captive," Richard G. Scott stated. "You are familiar with his strategy. He whispers: ... 'You can't change; you have tried before and failed.' 'It's too late; you've gone too far.' Don't let him discourage you. Freedom from your transgression will come through sincere faith, true repentance, willing obedience, and the giving of self. (See Alma 26:22)" *(Ensign, May 1990)*

True Repentance

Alma gave advice to his son Corianton which is an insightful formula for the repentance needed in the life of a transgressor.

•Remorse and Sorrow

Alma first wanted his son to feel remorse and sorrow for what he had done. "I would to God that ye had not been guilty of so great a crime," he tells him. "I would not dwell upon your crimes, *to harrow up your soul*, if it were not for your good." (Alma 39:7, italics added) Richard G. Scott advised, "Study and ponder to determine how serious the Lord defines your transgression to be. That will bring healing sorrow and remorse. It will also bring a sincere desire for change and a willingness to submit to every requirement for forgiveness." *(Ensign, May 1995)*

•Forsaking Sin

Alma then asks his son to abandon and forsake his sins. He said, "Repent and forsake your sins, and go no more after the lusts of your eyes, but cross yourself in all these things." (Alma 39:9) Richard G. Scott explained it this way:

Decide to stop what you are doing that is wrong. Then search out everything in your life that feeds the habit, such as negative thoughts, unwholesome environment, and your companions in mischief. Systematically eliminate or overcome everything that contributes to that negative part of your life. Then stop the negative things permanently.

Recognize that you'll go through two transition periods. The first is the most difficult. You are caging the tiger that has controlled your life. It will shake the bars, growl, threaten, and cause you some disturbance. But I promise you that this period will pass. How long it takes will depend upon the severity of your transgression, the strength of your determination, and the help you seek from the Lord. But remember, as you stand firm, it will pass.

The second period is not as intense. It is like being on "battle alert" so that you can fend off any enemy attack. That too will pass, and you will feel more and have increased control of your life. You will become free. (*Ensign*, May 1990)

In order to do this, "to cross yourself in these things," (Alma 39:10) Alma commands his son to "take it upon you to counsel in your undertakings; for...ye stand in need to be nourished by your brothers. And give heed to their counsel." (Alma 39:10) Giving heed to the counsel of loved ones and priesthood holders who are willing to give righteous direction is an essential part of gaining strength to forsake transgression completely. Often the counsel of trained professionals is needed, as well.

•Confession of Sin, Restitution for Sin

Alma then commands his son Corianton to "acknowledge your faults and that wrong which ye have done" with an admonition to return to those he had wronged with his confession. (Alma 39:13) Serious moral transgressions also need to be confessed to a stake president or bishop. Then, "You must restore as far as possible all that which is stolen, damaged or defiled," Richard G. Scott said. (*Ensign*, May 1995) Alma and the sons of Mosiah are a good example of this. They "traveled throughout all the land...*zealously striving to repair all the injuries they had done to the church*, confessing all their sins." (Mosiah 27:35, italics added) Boyd K. Packer once stated:

> But sometimes you *cannot* give back what you have taken because you don't have it to give. If you have caused others to suffer unbearably—defiled someone's virtue, for example—it is not within your power to give it back. ...Restoring what you cannot restore, healing the wound you cannot heal, fixing that which you broke and cannot fix is the very purpose of the atonement of Christ. (*Ensign*, Nov. 1995)

This statement leads to the last and most important step in the repentance process.

•Seeking the Savior

Alma issued the command to his son Corianton to "turn to the Lord with all your mind, might and strength." (Alma 39:13) Richard G. Scott advised:

> By understanding the Atonement, you will see that God is not a jealous being who delights in persecuting those who misstep. He is an absolutely perfect, compassionate, understanding, patient, and forgiving Father. He is willing to entreat, counsel, strengthen, lift, and fortify. He so loves each of us that He was willing to have his perfect, sinless, absolutely obedient, totally righteous Son experience indescribable agony and pain and give Himself in sacrifice for all. (*Ensign*, May 1995)

This principle can be illustrated from a story told in the *Ensign* by Frances Warden. The story is as follows:

> During the past several years, since the chain of events began that led to my divorce, I have experienced more sleepless nights and heartbroken prayers than at any other period of my life.
>
> ...One night in particular, I poured out my heart for well over an hour, overwhelmed by what I saw as the failures that had blighted my children's lives and led to their presence in a home without a father. During that dark hour, it seemed impossible to bear the conviction that I had destroyed something precious and had irreconcilably lost something vitally important to me and my children. I spent a restless night following my prayer, awakening at 2:00 A.M. still conversing in my mind about the subject of my earlier prayer.
>
> I knew Christ had died so that we might not bear the weight of our failures and guilt indefinitely, but I could not see how even my repentance and Christ's atonement could undo what had gone amiss in my own, my former husband's, and my children's lives. I thought, "The Lord himself has never injured anyone, as I have, through ignorance, selfishness, and poor judgment. He has never failed. He does not have to bear the incessant burden of knowing that he has damaged a love one's life."
>
> "Neither do you," came the quiet answer in my mind. I was suddenly flooded with the realization that when I accepted our Savior's sacrifice for my sins, he had taken them on his shoulders in a more real sense than I had ever before understood. Once I had repented of those sins and made what restitution I could, the matter of who had been at fault became irrelevant. The concern shifted from the past to the future. (*Ensign*, June 1988)

The Savior has said, "Remember the worth of souls is great in the sight of God. For, behold, the Lord your Redeemer suffered death in the flesh; wherefore he suffered the pain of all men, that all men might repent and come unto him. ...And how great is his joy in the soul that repenteth!" (D&C 18:10–13)

The Savior knows us personally and intimately. He knows our thoughts, weaknesses and vulnerabilities. He knows us so well He knows the number of hairs on our heads. (Luke 12:7) I believe He informs us of this fact to let us know that since He is aware of something so trivial, surely He is aware of everything of importance in our lives.

The Savior knows the burdens and pains of those who have transgressed. He knows the pains and heartaches of those who have been hurt by those transgressions. He can lead each respectively to healing and wholeness because of who He is and what He has experienced.

"Return Unto Me...That I May Heal You" (3 Nephi 9:13)

The Savior asks, "Will ye not now return unto me, and repent of your sins, and be converted, *that I may heal you?*" (3 Nephi 9:13, italics added) Boyd K. Packer related an experience that shows the healing and love the Savior has to offer. He said:

> Some years ago I was in Washington, D. C., with President Harold B. Lee. Early one morning he called me to come into his hotel room. He was sitting in his robe reading *Gospel Doctrine* by President Joseph F. Smith and he said, "Listen to this!
>
> "Jesus had not finished his work when his body was slain, neither did he finish it after his resurrection from the dead. ...And when will he? *Not until he has redeemed and saved every son and daughter of our father Adam that have been or ever will be born upon this earth to the end of time*, except the sons of perdition. That is his mission."
>
> And so we pray, and we fast, and we plead, and we implore. *We love those who wander, and we never give up hope.* (*Ensign*, Nov. 1995, italics added)

Those who love any who have fallen away into forbidden paths can ultimately rely on this promise—that the Savior will never give up on any of his beloved children and that He has already died and suffered for sins committed by them. He will give each person dealing with a straying loved one the insights necessary to do all that he or she can do to help a loved one come back to Him. He will then give promises, divine sustenance and the strength necessary to hold on in faith until those transgressors repent.

Since the Savior will never give up on someone He loves, He will give us each respectively the faith, hope, insights and eternal anchors necessary for us to never give up hope either. We can thus come to rely on the One who has paid the price for all sins to carry the burdens of our deep love and caring. We can know what to do for each and every son or daughter of God that will help that person become clean and whole again and through this knowledge find the peace necessary to continue on faithful in our own lives. The Savior thus becomes the key—the *only* key—to lasting healing and wholeness.

Extending the Arm of Mercy:

HEALING RELATIONSHIPS SCARRED BY INFIDELITY

1

"The Sobbings of Their Hearts Ascend Up to God Against You" (Jacob 2:35)

Sarah will never forget the moment her husband came to her and informed her that he had been untrue to their marriage and the sacred covenants made between them in the temple. She heard her husband's words with both shock and disbelief. Nothing had prepared her heart for the painful news he chose to share with her at that time.

It was not as if Sarah had been unaware of difficulties within her marriage. She had been. Her interaction with her husband, which had become more and more infrequent over the past several months, had often been strained and contentious. They seldom spoke and scarcely shared intimacy. It was as if they were only roommates, occupying the same home but not sharing anything personal between them.

For the past several months, too, her husband had distanced himself from the children, rarely interacting positively with them. He took no part in Family Nights or other family events. He was quick to discipline the children and reprimand them for the normal noises of family living. He seemed impatient and frustrated with their childish behaviors. They in turn had withdrawn from him and did not seek him out as they once had done.

Her husband had also shown a lack of commitment to the Church, failing to keep his home teaching assignments, not accepting callings because of his work schedule, and missing sacrament meetings often due to sickness or fatigue. All these changes in behavior were gradual, not drastic. They had occurred over time so nothing seemed significantly different to Sarah. She had attributed all of these behaviors—and her husband's obvious preoccupation with other matters—to difficulties her husband was experiencing at work and the repercussions of health problems he had dealt with over the past several months.

When Sarah first found out that her husband had been untrue to her, all she could do was sob uncontrollably. She not only felt hurt and devastated, she felt vulnerable and frightened. She had seen other close friends and relatives go through the ravages of infidelity, many whose relationships had been irreparably damaged, and now she could see the same thing happening within her own marriage. She had worked hard to avoid something such as this, but would her marriage now also end in divorce, as others had, despite all of her efforts and desires otherwise?

Sarah's husband had approached her and told her the truth because he claimed he could no longer stand leading the double life of deception he had been leading. He wanted to change and become clean again. He told Sarah he had no more desire to violate the commandments or break the covenants made between them. He wanted to attempt to heal their relationship and start anew, if they could.

His assertions and his attempts to conciliate did not help. Sarah couldn't escape the intense emotional trauma that had resulted from his confession. She felt hurt, angry, betrayed and full of deep misgiving. How could she trust anything her husband said or did now when he had made a previous commitment to be true to her and their marriage? If he had violated their covenants once, what was to stop him from violating those covenants again? What if her husband had become so entrenched in sin that he could not pull himself away from the destructive course he was on despite his desires to do so?

Sarah had witnessed enough from other relationships damaged by infidelity to know that the road ahead of them, if they did stay together, would be long, arduous, difficult and painful. She had known other couples who had attempted the journey but had not been able to make it. Too many forces had pulled them apart and they had not been able to heal. What if they became one of those couples? Even if they did end up staying together, was attempting to salvage their broken relationship worth the pain and anguish both she and the children would experience along the way?

During the first few days following her husband's confession, Sarah could scarcely function because of intense inward turmoil. She felt lost and alone, unable to confide in the one person she'd always been able to turn to in times of crisis before—her husband. She ate little and hardly slept. Her feelings often vacillated between hurt and anger and between intense loneliness and fear of what the future held for her and her family. She was consumed by a grief she'd never felt before.

Sarah cried often and found herself withdrawing even further from her husband, trying to protect her heart from any more pain and turmoil he might cause her. Although she wanted to express her feelings to him, she found she could not open up to him in any way. She distrusted how he would react, she distrusted him, and she felt certain he would treat her feelings with impatience, apathy and misunderstanding.

Sarah prayed fervently for divine help to know what to

do, to know how to move forward with her life at this crucial time. She turned in desperation to the Savior for whatever comfort or solace she could get from Him during these days of intense trial, pain and suffering. She grasped for any peace or hope He might have for her through the scriptures. She meticulously marked those that came to have meaning to her, reading and re-reading the ones which gave her much-needed comfort. She sought for divine direction from priesthood leaders and from priesthood blessings to know what to do with her life and with the lives of her children. She pleaded for the Lord's strength and His assistance to keep functioning effectively despite the heart-wrenching anguish she felt inside that almost immobilized her.

The Lord's answers came to her little by little, day by day, step by step as she turned completely to him and relinquished her will to His. Although Sarah considered the possibility of divorce, she felt strongly directed by the Spirit to stay with her husband and attempt the process of rebuilding their marriage. Even with this divine directive, she did not feel the certainty of whether or not her efforts would be effective or whether or not her marriage would ultimately be healed. She only felt that such a course was the Lord's desire for her at the present time and she wanted to move forward in faith, knowing she was aligning her will to the Lord's and doing what He would have her do at that time.

This step was not an easy step for her to take. Sarah had to deeply humble herself in order to move forward with her husband, knowing her marriage was still filled with contention and extreme difficulty. Although her husband had confessed to the bishop and had begun counseling with him, he still openly resented her for her lack of forgiveness and compassion for him and for the difficulties she had in moving forward with their relationship. He often became angry and impatient with her, even in front of the children, and continued to lay the blame for the majority of their marital problems on her. He often treated her with hostility and contempt, still criticizing her often, claiming she didn't have the appropriate concern, understanding and compassion for him that a wife should have.

During these difficult times, Sarah often felt the sustaining arms of the Savior around her as she was called upon to cope with the injustices that had come about in her life because of her husband's transgressions. She felt the oft-repeated assurance she was deeply loved when she found no similar assurance from her spouse or her marriage. As she dealt with her husband's continuing contentious behavior, she felt the unquestioning love of the Savior buoy and strengthen her enough to stay with him and within their marriage.

With the Savior's continued help, sustenance and insights, she was ultimately able to begin to deal with her tempestuous relationship and slowly begin the process of healing. These efforts taxed everything she had inside—her ability to love, her ability to forgive and her ability to go on when she had none of her own strength left, only a determination to do what the Lord required of her. When Sarah became incapable of dealing with the negative repercussions of her husband's actions, she would turn to the Lord in yearning prayer and plead for His sustaining help. He never failed her. Sometimes when she felt as if she would collapse, He would step in and help her until she had the strength and faith to begin to move forward again.

Not only did the Lord send divine comfort, He brought people into Sarah's life who understood, strengthened and upheld her through these difficult times. He gave her continued direction and comfort through priesthood blessings which became an anchor and lifeline to her in her darkest, bleakest hours.

A turning point for Sarah came when she was told through a priesthood blessing that she had been "foreordained" to help her husband and that this had been a calling given to her from the Lord. The Lord told her the time had come to help her husband repent, to call him to repentance "in humility, not haughtiness." She was promised that if she would do this, her husband would feel the power of her words through the Holy Ghost and know she was speaking the will of the Lord. Although the Lord told her He would not reveal the end of what would happen in their marriage because of free agency, He promised that He would be in front of her and that legions of angels would surround her, angels who were willing and able to help sustain her and her family if she would only but ask.

Sarah began to feel powerful spiritual confidence in her Savior because of these experiences. Her trust in Him, as Enos's, "began to be unshaken." (Enos 1:11) She came to understand that even if she and her husband did separate, the Savior would take care of her in every way. The Savior became her anchor and lifeline, her one source of peace. With this anchor, Sarah knew she could take every feeling, emotion, problem and hardship to the Lord. She began to realize that as her life centered on Him, her own spiritual and emotional healing began taking place. As she became stronger, more whole and healthy herself, she could, from this strength, better reach out to her husband in helping him repent, in being patient with his slow but discernible progress and in handling the verbal attacks, anger and hostility that still came from him. She began to learn how to see and effectively deal with her husband's continuing rationalizations for the sins he'd committed.

Over time, Sarah noticed small differences in their relationship. Her husband became less angry and impatient with her and began to make changes in his own personal life that showed his heart had begun to soften. He started spending more time at home and with the children, he became more active in church callings and he treated Sarah with more kindness and less anger and impatience.

These positive steps would continue for awhile and then suddenly it seemed they would backtrack completely, as if starting over. The same cycle of anger, impatience, rationalization, blame and hostility would arise and Sarah would wonder if they'd made any progress at all or if she'd just imagined it. Each time she would fall back on the Savior, who would succor and strengthen her, giving the peace she needed to keep trying. Sarah and her husband would move forward again until they would fall into a difficult cycle once more. She noticed, however, that the difficult cycles seemed to be lessening in intensity, they seemed to last for a shorter duration and they became less frequent.

Because of Sarah's faithful endurance and her husband's willingness to try to makes changes and repent of his wrongdoing, they were ultimately able to begin to rebuild their relationship, a relationship which has become more meaningful to them. Now, years later, Sarah expresses a gratitude to the Savior for sustaining her in a marriage she once thought she wanted no part of. She loves her husband and feels he has better come to understand and have compassion for all the trials and tribulations she went through in order to keep their marriage intact.

Despite the pain of dealing with the past, Sarah feels eternally grateful for what she experienced through her trials. She feels that the insights and strengths gained from these hardships have not only been beneficial in terms of her own spiritual strength and growth but she feels these experiences have made her marriage even more meaningful to her. She knows that even if her marriage ended and her husband left her—as she saw happen to friends and family members, she could still find wholeness and safety in the Savior. Her trust and faith in the Savior has been strengthened far beyond what she ever imagined because of these experiences. She knows the Savior literally carried her through the difficult times and she knows and trusts that He will now carry her through whatever difficulties befall her in her life. Sarah has come to deeply cherish the divine statement from the Lord in which He said, "Behold, and lo, I am with the faithful *always*." (D&C 62:9, italics added)

2

"These are They Who...Overcome By Faith"
(D&C 76:51-53)

As infidelity becomes an ever-increasing problem both within and without the Church, many will deal with a situation very similar to what Sarah had to deal with in the last chapter—the uncertainty of whether to attempt to move forward and heal a relationship marred by infidelity or terminate that marriage and divorce an unfaithful spouse because of the damage done to the relationship. This section is aimed primarily at those who have chosen to remain in a damaged marital relationship and move forward toward healing. It needs to be understood that although someone may sincerely desire to heal a broken marriage despite all the pain and anguish a spouse has caused, that person might not be granted the opportunity to do so. Often those who have chosen to be unfaithful to the marriage covenants also choose, because of free agency, to terminate a marriage.

Those who do stay in a relationship in which infidelity in any form has occurred face a road which is long, arduous, painful and difficult. The trials that have come and that will continue to come will be some of the most painful, taxing and agonizing trials that person will ever face. Inherent worth will be questioned, self-confidence will be tried, and the ability to endure and overcome in faith will be tested to the utmost. Only those who have the sustaining power of the Savior will make it through these trying times of darkness and uncertainty.

It is no wonder that the Lord gives repeated warnings about the serious repercussions of infidelity and the severe consequences of participating in it. The damage done by infidelity is far-reaching and devastating not only to victims, their families and extended families but to perpetrators, as well. The healing process needed to repair damaged relationships is done in terms of *months and years*, not days and weeks. This healing process, however, has occurred in many relationships scarred by infidelity.

Some years ago one stake president, who had been counseling with a woman who faced divorce because of her husband's infidelity, told her that at that time he was dealing with her situation, he was also dealing with one hundred and six similar cases to her own in their stake. Out of all of these couples, only three couples had divorced. That meant one hundred and three couples, besides those who had not yet come forward, had struggled through the devastation of either emotional or physical infidelity and had chosen to stay together. They had been forced to deal with the negative ramifications of a spouse's sinful behavior but had been able—or were working desperately—to overcome it. Many stake presidents and bishops can testify to the fact that numbers have only increased over time. More and more are placed on the front lines in the battle against sexual sin.

Despite the hardships faced by those who are trying to overcome the painful consequences of infidelity, many who have worked to overcome it express their gratitude and deep love for a Savior who helped carry their burdens and who helped heal their broken hearts. They know the eternal consequences of their choices are endless—for them, for their children and for their future posterity.

Melanie, a woman who agonized over a father who had

committed adultery and the devastating effects his sins had on
her mother, knew it would be years before healing occurred in
her parents' marriage—if, of course, healing did occur at all.
Melanie felt troubled over the burdens her mother would be
called upon to carry if she chose to stay within the marriage and
work out the problems her father's sins had created between
them. *Would this be wasted time?* Melanie wondered. *Would it
be worthwhile for her mother to deal with the pain and
hardship of her father's sins or would it be better for her to
leave him and forge a new life on her own, a life where she
might not have to deal with so much heartache, a life not filled
with so much contention, anxiety and uncertainty, a life where
she might find someone who loved, cherished and respected her
unlike her father currently did?*

One night as Melanie thought over the situation, she felt
deeply impressed that even if her parents' marriage did take
years to heal, that this was a minimal portion of their lives here
on this earth and in reality a tiny blip in relation to the eternities.
She felt she could almost envision in her mind the timeline of
her parents' lives here on earth and then see that time in relation
to eternity—the tiny glitch in time it would take for them to
overcome the problems they would experience because of her
father's transgressions. It seemed but a "small moment." (D&C
121:7) From this experience, Melanie learned that the Lord cared
far more about the eternal consequences of her parents'
decisions rather than the fact that it might take years to heal
their scarred relationship. Even if it did take earthly time to
recover spiritual ground, this time would be worth it in relation
to the eternities. Melanie understood that "the eternal purposes
of the Lord shall roll on, until all his promises shall be
fulfilled." (Mormon 8:22) Melanie could then support her mother
through the horrendous trials that came until the Lord could

work the miracle of His healing in her parents' lives.

"With Me Ye Shall Find Rest" (3 Nephi 28:3)

Many couples in marriages similar to this have gone through tremendous hardships but have ultimately been able to restore their relationships. Despite the weighty trials they have faced in trying to overcome infidelity, with the Lord's help these marriages have truly become stronger and fulfilling to both parties involved. Many spouses who have put their partners through the debilitating effects of their sins have come to see the truth about the mistakes of the past and have been "convinced of the error which they are in." (3 Nephi 1:25) They have come to accept the blame and responsibility for their actions instead of repeatedly blaming their spouses for all of their past behaviors and indiscretions. They truly have become "redeemed of the Lord," in that they are "delivered from that endless night of darkness." (Alma 41:7) Many who have strayed, too, have come to see how the intense marital problems they have dealt with in their marriages were a result of their transgressions and mistakes, not their spouses' doings, behaviors, actions or attitudes.

"All Things Wherewith You Have Been Afflicted Shall Work Together For Your Good, and to My Name's Glory" (D&C 98:3)

These types of successes in healing marriages can only come about through enduring faith in the Savior. Most often it is the one who has stayed committed to the marriage—the one who has been betrayed—who will bear the greatest burden in keeping such a marriage together. He or she will be called upon to carry many unjust burdens during the process of trying to heal. Victims will experience pain, hardship, agony and turmoil during this process. They will be attacked, belittled, undermined or mocked as those who have transgressed make rationalizations for sinful behavior. They will be objects of anger, ridicule, criticism and blame as the responsibility for marital problems will be thrust solely on them.

Many spouses who have transgressed harbor deep, almost uncontrollable anger for partners who have remained committed to the marriage covenant. This anger has been fed, cultivated and worked upon by Satan to form the basis for rationalizations used to justify sinful behaviors. This anger does not disappear when a straying spouse decides to come back to a marriage. This anger has to be dissolved step by step, line by line, idea by idea and effort by effort. Until it is dissolved, the committed spouse will fall victim to the venom of this type of thinking and the resulting behaviors from it.

It is only those who have the sustaining power of the Savior who will be able to make it through these difficult times. Only those who tap into the Savior's gifts of love, patience and longsuffering will be able to find the ability to forgive a partner who has betrayed them and who often continues to betray them with anger, hostility, contention or blame. Only those who are blessed with the Savior's insights and strength will gather the fortitude necessary to help them discern and overcome the thought patterns and rationalizations that brought a partner down to the depths of sin in the first place.

Furthermore, only those who are buoyed by the Savior's unconditional love will maintain the self-confidence and self-worth needed to fend off the attacks and barbs that will come from straying parties, attacks that may hit upon their deepest vulnerabilities and insecurities. Only those who feel the Savior's peace and comfort amidst times of intense trial will be able to move forward and heal any relationships scarred by infidelity. They need this sustaining strength from the Savior to endure a lifestyle in which everything outside them causes them to question inherent worth.

This type of endurance cannot be mistaken for becoming victims of abusive, manipulative, demeaning or controlling behaviors. It is endurance based upon putting up with temporary blindness when a transgressor is trying to overcome sin. When there is persistent sin, harassment or continued, unabated abuse, these cannot be tolerated or ignored—which can mean the dissolution of a relationship. However, the blessings of enduring and overcoming in faith can be realized as transgressing spouses make choices to let go of darkness and cleave once again to the covenants he or she has made. This can and does happen—and has before.

Steven A. Cramer in *The Worth of a Soul* attributes his ability to overcome his sins of infidelity to his wife's gifts of enduring patience given to her from the Savior. In one part of his book, he describes the process of overcoming his sins this way:

> My escape from Satan's power was not as sudden as Alma's, who in the very instance of recognizing Christ in his life was relieved of his anguish and filled with unspeakable joy, peace, and forgiveness. (See Alma 36:1-24) But my rescue was just as real and wonderful as his was. Slowly, purposefully, step-by-step, the Lord began to work the miracles of His rescue and salvation in my life. Line upon line, never faster than I could receive it, He began directing the proper help into my life. He made me aware of truths I had never recognized before. He began to open scriptures to my understanding which built my faith in Him. He raised up friends to help. *He awakened me to a life of joy and peace that I had never in my wildest imaginations thought possible.* (p. 96, italics added)

Only the enduring faith and patience of the wronged spouse will bring about this great miracle of healing in the lives of those who have betrayed them. As mentioned before, this faith and patience will only come as gifts from the Lord and Savior who loves us more deeply than we will ever come to fully understand in this life. These gifts of faith and patience can and will come, however, to those who seek them in righteousness. The Lord has promised that He will deliver us from any type of bondage when we humble ourselves before Him and "[cry] mightily unto him. Thus doth the Lord work with his power *in all cases* among the children of men, extending the arm of mercy towards them that put their trust in him." (Mosiah 29:20, italics added)

3

"I Prepare You Against These Things" (Ether 2:25)

The preparation for and journey of the brother of Jared and his people across the "great deep" towards the Promised Land can be a symbolic representation of the journey required of one who chooses to stay within a marriage scarred by infidelity. (Ether 2:25) The Lord tells the brother of Jared before his long journey: "For behold, ye shall be as a whale in the midst of the sea; for the mountain waves shall dash upon you. Nevertheless, I will bring you up again out of the depths of the sea." (Ether 2:24) In other words, this journey—the journey of one traveling the long road toward healing a relationship scarred by infidelity—will be filled with trials, anguish, hardship and difficulties, for indeed, "the mountain waves shall dash upon you." Nevertheless, the Lord will "bring you up again out of the depths of the sea"—that is, He will comfort, sustain, guide and direct those whose wills are aligned with His through each of these trials. (Ether 2:24)

The Lord, for the Jaredites, touched sixteen small stones that "that they may shine forth in darkness" (Ether 3:4) so that the Jaredites "might not cross the great waters in darkness." (Ether 6:3) The Lord will give this light to anyone making a similar journey as long as they turn to Him in faith. "They did have light continually, whether it was above the water or under the water," the scriptures tell us. (Ether 6:10) In other words, the Lord gave light continually whether there were outside events of hardship

153

or whether it remained calm.

Through the hard times that *will* come, the Lord will give anchors of strength and light through the scriptures, through the counsel of righteous priesthood holders and through priesthood blessings, through personal revelation and through the words and actions of righteous people. "I am he; yea, I am he that comforteth you," He reminds us. (2 Nephi 8:12) In order to get this comfort, those who journey must, as the Jaredites did, go forth "commending themselves unto the Lord their God." (Ether 6:4) They must trust Him implicitly that the path He has for them—even if it is hard—is the best for them, although they cannot see the end of His ways or know the end of the path they are on. They must trust that even if this journey continues to be painful, difficult and rocky, the Lord will never leave them alone but give them compensatory blessings to overcome the consequences of acts that were not their own. The scriptures state:

> [The Jaredites] were many times buried in the depths of the sea, because of the mountain waves which broke upon them, and also the great and terrible tempests which were caused by the fierceness of the wind.
>
> ...When they were encompassed about by many waters they did cry unto the Lord, *and he did bring them forth again upon the top of the waters.*
> (Ether 6:6-7, italics added)

Thus it is for those dealing with difficulties in their marriages caused by the infidelity of a spouse. When hardships become "great and terrible," when persons dealing with these situations are "encompassed about" by trials, heartache and turmoil, they may cry unto the Lord and He will bring them "forth again upon the top of the waters." (Ether 6:7) He will give them the peaceful reassurance that He is near them, guiding them, walking with them and sustaining them in every step of their journey. In other words, outward events of turmoil and hardship will not destroy the inward peace the Savior can—and will—give.

The Jaredites set off on a journey in which they did not know the end or the duration. They only had the promise from the Lord in which He said, "There will I meet thee, and I will go before thee into a land which is choice above all the lands of the earth." (Ether 1:42) Those dealing with infidelity in a marriage have a similar promise. The Lord has said, "I will go before your face. I will be on your right hand and on your left, and my Spirit shall be in your hearts, and mine angels round about you, to bear you up." (D&C 84:88)

Those who learn to walk with the Savior will, as the Jaredites did as they reached the Promised Land, bow "themselves down...and...humble themselves before the Lord, and...shed tears of joy before the Lord, because of the multitude of his tender mercies over them." (Ether 6:12) Many who have dealt with relationships damaged by infidelity have testified of the Lord's tender mercies and His sustaining power through their trials. They testify of the Savior's promise when He said, "I will not leave you comfortless; *I will come to you.*" (John 14:18, italics added) They have come to know they will never be left alone to deal with what has befallen them because of the transgressions of others but they will always have an eternal source of comfort, love and peace to buoy and strengthen them as they move forward in faith.

One woman who had gone through intense difficulties in her marriage said, "I didn't know I could go through what I did. I didn't know I had the capacity to do so. But never in my life have I felt the Savior so near to me. I've never felt the Spirit as near me since that time, but that's because I haven't needed it as much as I believe I did then."

Another woman going through similar trials told of an experience she had one night as the burdens she carried became too great for her to bear. Late into the night as she carried the burdens of her husband's infidelity and the added burden of the sickness of a child, she fell to her knees and sobbed. "I couldn't do it anymore," she said. "I couldn't go on. As I cried and prayed, I literally felt the arms of the Savior around me, comforting me and hugging me. It was as tangible as anything I've ever felt. After that experience, I knew He would help me whenever I needed Him. I knew I was not alone."

This woman had been, as others will who face similar trials, "encircled about eternally in the arms of [the Savior's] love." (1 Nephi 1:15) The Lord tells us, "Therefore, fear not, little flock; do good; let earth and hell combine against you, for if ye are built upon my rock, *they cannot prevail.*" (D&C 6:34, italics added)

"The Lord in his great infinite goodness doth bless and prosper those who put their trust in him," we have been told. (Helaman 12:1) As the prophet Jacob reminded those in his time who were suffering the effects of their spouses' infidelity, "Look unto God with firmness of mind, and pray unto him with exceeding faith, and he will console you in your afflictions, and he will plead your cause, and send down justice upon those who seek your destruction. O all ye that are pure in heart, lift up your heads and receive the pleasing word of God, and feast upon his love; for ye may, if your minds are firm, forever." (Jacob 3:1-2)

4

"He That Repents Not, From Him Shall Be Taken Even the Light Which He Has Received" (D&C 1:33)

Many who deal with infidelity initially feel prompted of the Lord to stay within their marriages but are surprised and shocked when, after these powerful impressions and their efforts to follow them, their marriages do not work out. *Why, they might wonder, would the Lord have given those types of promptings when their marriages didn't heal but still failed? Wouldn't that be the only reason the Lord would have directed them this way, to stay with a sinning spouse who had hurt and betrayed them—and one who continued to hurt them—because He wanted their marriages to last? Then why didn't they?*

Before the final battle in which the Nephites were swept from off the face of the earth, after they had "dwindle[d] in unbelief and wickedness from year to year," (4 Nephi 1:34) the Lord commanded Mormon to cry repentance unto his people once again. The Lord was giving the Nephite people one final chance to "build up again my church" and "be spared." (Mormon 3:2) This would become their last opportunity to return to Him and become whole again. Mormon tells us, "I did cry unto this people, but it was in vain; and they did not realize that it was the Lord that had spared them, and granted unto them a chance for repentance." They, therefore, "did harden their hearts against the Lord their God." (Mormon 3:3)

As often happens in relationships where infidelity

157

occurs, the Lord may prompt those who have stayed true to a marriage to continue within the partnership and give the marriage a second chance. This does not guarantee that the relationship will heal. It often indicates that the Lord is granting unto the straying party one last chance for repentance. Though this opportunity might be rejected, the Lord often "doth suffer that they may do this thing, or that the people may do this thing unto them, according to the hardness of their hearts, *that the judgments which he shall exercise upon them in his wrath might be just.*" (Alma 14:11, italics added) In other words, sinning parties are granted another chance for repentance that "they are left without excuse, and their sins are upon their own heads." (D&C 88:82)

The Lord has said, "In his hot displeasure, and in his fierce anger, in his time," He will "cut off those wicked unfaithful, and unjust stewards, and appoint them their portion among hypocrites, and unbelievers. Pray ye, therefore, that their ears may be opened unto your cries, that I may be merciful unto them, that these things may not come upon them." (D&C 101:90-93) The Lord will do all that He can, without taking away free agency, to give us opportunities to repent and become clean again. Even if these opportunities are rejected by those who have sinned, it does not mean the Lord has not been working His will. It means that those who have transgressed "perceive not the light, and they turn their hearts from me." (D&C 45:29) They have "harden[ed] their hearts against the Holy Spirit, that it hath no place in them." (2 Nephi 33:2)

Ben, who discovered his wife had participated in an adulterous affair, felt strongly directed of the Lord to stay with his wife in their marriage. This was not an easy thing for him to accept or an easy decision for him to make. His wife had been involved in adultery with his best friend and besides this deeply hurting him, the two of them together continued to attack, belittle, undermine and condemn him, claiming his behaviors drove his wife to infidelity, that he was the cause of any marital problems and that he was self-centered, emotionally unhealthy, manipulative, dysfunctional and full of deceit.

Still, after a week of intense prayer, fasting, agonizing deliberation and soul-searching, Ben knew the Lord wanted him to return to his wife and attempt to heal their marriage. With deep humility and with every intention of taking his wife back, trying to forgive past hurts and move toward healing their marriage, he returned home. Ben had supposed that due to his deep spiritual impressions to return to his wife, his wife's heart would be similarly softened and that she would be repentant and making simultaneous gestures to heal and patch up their marriage. This was not the case. His wife almost seemed angry and vengeful that he had returned, as if she had hoped her revelations of betrayal would give him cause to leave her. Because they had not, she continued her barrage of criticism and degradation, claiming she would be much happier if he was out of her life, that he made her miserable, and that he was truly all these bad things she had come to believe and see about him. She made unreasonable and constant demands of him, trying to force him to act in "such and such a way" in order for her to even try to live with him again.

Even as Ben did try to make these efforts, they were never enough for her. She continued to find fault with him constantly, never letting up on her criticism, anger or hostility. Not long after this, Ben came to find out his wife and his best friend were filing for divorce in both of their marriages and moving toward their own marriage. Despite their claims to give their marriages a second chance, they had never once intended to try to work out their problems or remain with their current spouses. Despite knowing this, Ben also knew he had been directed of the Lord to continue with his wife during that time. He came to believe that the Lord was giving his wife one last chance to "purge ye out the iniquity which is among you." (D&C 43:11)

Those who have sinned will suffer the punishment of God unless they repent. Though this suffering might not be immediate, "what I the Lord have decreed...shall be fulfilled." (D&C 1:7) The Lord has said:

> Wo be unto this people, for I have seen their abominations, and their wickedness, and their whoredoms; and except they repent I will visit them in mine anger.
>
> They shall know that I am the Lord their God, and am a jealous God, visiting the iniquities of my people.
>
> Except this people repent and turn unto the Lord their God, they shall be brought into bondage; and none shall deliver them, except it be the Lord the Almighty God.
>
> Yea, and it shall come to pass when they shall cry unto me I will be slow to hear their cries; yea, and I will suffer them that they be smitten by their enemies.
>
> And except they repent in sackcloth and ashes, and cry mightily to the Lord their God, I will not hear their prayers, neither will I deliver them out of their afflictions. (Mosiah 11:20, 22-25)

The Lord has also said:

> How often would I have gathered you together as a hen gathereth her chickens under her wings, but ye would not! How oft have I called upon you by the mouth of my servants, and by the ministering of angels, and by mine own voice...and by the great sound of a trump, and by the voice of judgment, and by the voice of mercy all the day long, and by the voice of glory and honor and the riches of

eternal life, and would have saved you with an everlasting salvation, *but ye would not.* (D&C 43:24-25, italics added)

But "for all this," the Lord reminds us, "[my] anger is not turned away, but [my] hand is stretched out still." (2 Nephi 15:25) The Lord will wait unendingly for those He loves to return to Him. He will do everything in His power, without taking away free agency, to help sinning parties come back to the fold. Then if they do return to Him, the Lord has promised that "he that repents and does the commandments of the Lord *shall be forgiven.*" (D&C 1:32, italics added)

5

"Blessed Are They Who Humble Themselves Without Being Compelled to Be Humble" (Alma 32:16)

Two vastly different scenarios occur in relationships in which infidelity has been a part. The first scenario is similar to Sarah's situation in Chapter One of this section where her husband came to her with the intent and desire to confess, heal and become whole again—and to heal their marriage in the process. This type of situation is by far the most favorable in making efforts to repair a marriage because "he that truly humbleth himself, and repenteth of his sins, and endureth to the end, the same shall be blessed—yea, much more blessed than they who are compelled to be humble," the scriptures tell us. (Alma 32:15) This does not mean the situation will be easy but it does mean the Lord can work His hand in the relationship and help those parties involved "overcome through patience." (D&C 63:66) The Lord will help them step by step through the difficulties that will come as they try to move forward toward wholeness together. The Lord has said, "I, the Lord, forgive sins unto those who confess their sins before me and ask forgiveness, who have not sinned unto death." (D&C 64:7)

"There Were Among You Adulterers and Adulteresses... That Hereafter Shall Be Revealed" (D&C 63:14)

The second type of scenario that occurs after infidelity is far more difficult to overcome. This type of situation occurs when a party is discovered or caught in transgressions and in "secret works of darkness," (Helaman 10:3) where that person had no intent to confess but planned on continuing behaviors, possibly indefinitely. "Their works are in the dark; and they say: Who seeth us, and who knoweth us?" (2 Nephi 27:27) It is only after they are discovered that they find they must make a choice between their current partners or continuing on in the lifestyles they have chosen.

Often a sinning party is angry when he or she is brought to this point. Sinning parties often try to thrust the blame for their wicked behaviors on their spouses. They may claim their spouses have "never given them the love and attention they deserve" or have "never been there for them" or are "incapable of a healthy, loving relationship," thus attempting to justify themselves in pursuing the outside associations they've had.

Often, too, as those who have remained true to a marriage are coming to terms with the shock and resulting vulnerability of a betrayal, sinning parties will attack, criticize, and condemn their partners to an even greater extent, "enlarg[ing] the wounds of those who are already wounded." (Jacob 2:9) Sinning parties often cause those who have stayed committed to a marriage to go through times of deep emotional trauma as they subject them to rejection and continuing abuses.

It is easy to understand why when someone finds out about the unfaithful behavior of a partner that person wants to flee from a situation where he or she has been lied to, hurt, betrayed, mocked and rejected in everything shared with a spouse—everything from physical intimacy and emotional attachment to time, effort and past experiences together. Many have raised children together. Many have shared fulfilling relationships and wonderful memories. But everything they have shared, in essence, has been "turn[ed] aside" for a "thing of naught" (2 Nephi 28:16)—in other words, betrayed and rejected as something of no value.

The hurt one feels from this rejection is deep, pervasive and far-reaching, making some question even their worth. Many suffer guilt, anxiety and depression as they try to come to terms with what has happened to them. Some may even wonder if their spouses' attacks against them are justified or if indeed they were instrumental in driving their spouses away. Many accept the blame a spouse tries to thrust upon them when, in reality, they should not be accepting blame for a partner's sins.

Even if blame is not accepted, committed spouses still often cannot comprehend that suddenly someone they have spent many years with and made sacred covenants with would suddenly have a complete loss of caring, concern and compassion for them. They can barely fathom that their partners could "[make] a mock of that which was sacred" by tossing aside their eternal covenants as something of "no worth" to them. (2 Nephi 9:51)

One might question the Lord and His purposes when He directs such people to stay within a relationship that has caused pain, anguish and turmoil, a relationship in which they have suffered "much afflictions and much sorrow, because of the rudeness" of their spouses, (2 Nephi 2:1) a relationship full of deep mistrust, misgiving and uncertainty. It is a great leap of faith and trust for those people to stay within such a type of relationship if the Lord thus directs. Nothing from their relationship will initially give them any indication that such a step is worthwhile. They will still remain subjected to the evil behaviors of their straying spouses. They will be subjected to criticism, blame, antagonism, animosity and hostility. They will continue to be mistreated, hurt, misjudged, attacked and rejected.

Many on the outside who will see and watch this unjust

suffering and the hurt these people go through will adopt the thinking that, "It's better that you go on with your life. Move away from this person who has hurt and betrayed you and who has done so much damage to you and your family. Go on; you can do better. It is best that you move on." Though this is sometimes the Lord's directive, often it is not. Often the Lord wants those who have been hurt, betrayed and wounded to remain with that relationship to make efforts toward healing and reparation. This is a step that takes great sacrifice, faith and trust in the Savior and His ways in order to bear the unjust burdens that will come as they do His will in this way.

Those who are thus directed to stay essentially become the key—the only key—to possible healing. Steven A. Cramer said it this way: "When a branch is cut off from a tree, both the tree and the branch are injured. *If the wounds are ever to be healed, it will depend greatly on how the family responds to the unjust suffering this person will inflict upon them.*" (*The Worth of a Soul*, p. 56, italics added)

Sometimes the Lord allows us to suffer unjustly for the behaviors of others in an attempt to follow His will. It does not mean He takes that suffering lightly. It does not mean wicked behaviors will be unaccounted for or dismissed. It does mean that the Lord sees the bigger picture and what can happen in the future and He directs us accordingly. Richard G. Scott has said:

> This life is an experience in profound trust. ...To trust means to obey willingly without knowing the end from the beginning [see Prov. 3:5-7]. To produce fruit, your trust in the Lord must be more powerful and enduring than your confidence in your own personal feelings and experience.
> True enduring happiness with the accompanying strength, courage, and capacity to overcome the most challenging difficulties comes from a life centered in Jesus Christ. ...There is no

guarantee of overnight results, but there is absolute assurance that, in the Lord's time, solutions will come, peace will prevail, and emptiness will be filled. (*Ensign*, Nov. 1995)

It is a great and overwhelming undertaking to take upon the responsibility and burdens necessary to begin to heal a relationship scarred by infidelity. It is a trial of deep faith and commitment to do the Lord's will if such a thing is required, a trial that will tax every Christian virtue one has. Because the Lord knows that the key to healing a broken relationship often lies through the instrumentality of those who have been betrayed, through faith these people can be given the added capacity and strength to move forward in the way He asks. As they do this, Richard G. Scott reminds us:

> Please learn that as you wrestle with a challenge and feel sadness because of it, you can simultaneously have peace and rejoicing. Yes, pain, disappointment, frustration and anguish can be temporary scenes played out on the stage of life. Behind them there can be a background of peace and the positive assurance that a loving Father will keep His promises. (*Ensign*, Nov. 1995)

The Lord has promised the faithful, "I am with you to bless you and *deliver you* forever." (D&C 108:8, italics added) The Lord will never forget the righteous efforts of the faithful and, "in the midst of persecution and wickedness," (D&C 99: 1) He will give those following His will "peace to [their] souls" and "great faith," causing them that they might "hope for [their] deliverance in him." (Alma 58:11)

6

"I Would Exhort You to Come Unto Christ"
(Moroni 10:30)

Many who are faced with the prospect of healing a broken marriage do not even know where to begin. They may feel lost, alone, forsaken, overwhelmed and frightened at what lies ahead. They may be carrying burdens of grief, hurt, anguish and pain too great for them to bear, burdens that make it impossible to move forward in their lives. As said many times before, the key to healing any relationship scarred by infidelity is found in the Savior—in His power, in His love, in His forgiveness, in His patience, in His compassion, caring and mercy—and in His ability to carry the burdens He has successfully carried already. The Savior is the key; He is the only key to healing marriages scarred by infidelity.

In order for the Savior to work His miracle of healing in any relationship, both parties in that relationship must first find the Savior's healing in their own respective lives before any type of healing may be done in the relationship. This is an essential step in the healing process. One important element needs to be remembered during this process. *Even if one party fails to find the Savior and heal with Him, it does not mean the other party cannot find this healing and center his or her life on the One who will give that person the necessary comfort, sustenance, strength and anchors of promised eternal blessings to move forward in faith—no matter what path lies ahead.*

The covenants we make with the Savior and a spouse form a triangular pattern. Even if two sides of the triangle are broken due to the transgressions of another party, the other person is still sealed in a covenant relationship with the Savior. *This sealing has not been broken because of the sinful actions of a spouse.* The Savior is still there to comfort, sustain, lift, carry, direct, teach and guide those who are faithful to Him. His promises are sure and will not fail but "must be fulfilled." (D&C 109:44)

One woman recalled a time in her relationship that had been marred by considerable difficulty and distrust because of her husband's sexual sins. The problems between her and her husband had grown and become exacerbated to the point that she and her husband could scarcely talk for even a few moments without exchanging contentious words of anger, animosity and bitterness. They began to avoid each other so they wouldn't have to interact. They began to essentially coexist, not sharing anything intimate or personal. There were feelings of brooding anger and hostility that always seemed to lie just below the surface that would now and then resurface in bitter confrontations.

A loving and watchful elder's quorum president was guided through the Spirit to speak to this couple. He took them both aside individually, letting them express their feelings, views, past resentments and problems, and then he spoke to them together as a priesthood leader. He said, in essence, "My father was a bishop and counseled me to be very careful with any advice I give pertaining to a marriage relationship. However, in your case, I have felt strong impressions of what the Lord would have me say to you. I feel what both of you are trying to do is work on your relationship from where you're at. That can't be done right now. There are too many wounds and

170

too many hurt feelings. I feel impressed to counsel both of you to turn to the Lord individually. After you've found your personal healing with Him, He will then be able to make your relationship become whole because you will be moving forward with Him together." This man then blessed their marriage through the priesthood before he left.

Both the woman and this man subsequently took this advice to heart and began to reach for the Savior in their individual lives. The process of healing was slow and gradual but truly miraculous. As each of them began to center their lives on the Savior and become whole through Him, from this strength they could begin to look outward from their own once-tight shells and help each other. Because they became more secure within themselves and their own lives because of the Savior's healing power, each of them could then better understand the views, past hurts and vulnerabilities of the other. The Savior slowly led them step by step toward a greater healing. It was truly a refining time for them and their marriage and gave them defining keys that would help them with whatever trials of life would befall them—individually or together.

"Blessed Be God, Who Comforteth Us in All Our Tribulation" (2 Corinthians 1:3-4)

Victims of infidelity will go through a grieving process because of the losses they have experienced. There will be sorrow, tears, anguish and loneliness for what has been destroyed. There will be sleepless nights, turmoil, hardship and pain. There will be agonizing deliberation over what steps should be taken in the future for them and their families. There will be times of great anger and indignation against those who have sinned and caused so much damage and heartache. Victims truly do carry the burdens of others' sinful actions and are often called upon to carry the burdens of healing relationships scarred by them as well.

The Lord is aware of these burdens. He knows and has felt them before. He reminds us often to turn to Him, to lay these burdens at His feet that they "may be light." (Alma 33:23) He will not leave us alone as we accept of these burdens from Him. In a priesthood blessing given to a woman who was directed to stay with her unfaithful husband, the Lord told her to lay her every care upon Him. He assured her He knew that the burdens she'd been called upon to carry were heavy and unjust but that He'd asked that she accept these. The Savior reminded her that He too knew what it was like to carry the unjust burdens of others' sins. He also promised her He would never forget the burdens she bore for Him and that one day she would be compensated for all the burdens placed unfairly upon her shoulders.

Because of this woman's faithful trust in the Savior, her marriage was able to stay together. Her husband has often thanked her since that time for the efforts she made on his behalf. He has told her she was instrumental in saving him from his sins, that she has been a light and example to him and that he will forever be grateful for her loving endurance that helped their marriage become better.

> Behold, he who has repented of his sins, the same is forgiven, and I, the Lord, remember them no more. (D&C 58:42)

> Gird up your loins and be faithful, and ye shall overcome all things, and be lifted up at the last day. (D&C 75:22)

7

Moving Forward With a Broken Relationship

In *The Worth of a Soul,* Steven A. Cramer adequately describes the sensitive relationship that occurs between a husband and wife after there has been a betrayal. Although his description is based on his and his wife's relationship after his excommunication, it is representative of the feelings that can occur after there has been infidelity in any form:

> The old ways of relating won't work anymore. There are new wounds on both sides—deep wounds. Feelings are tender. Both partners are filled with doubts about the future, doubts about loyalties, doubts about how much they can depend on each other, doubts about the sincerity of repentance, doubts about the honesty of the forgiveness for the wrong which has come between them, doubts about their ability to understand and cope with the stress which has come into their relationship.
>
> ...At the beginning, my wife and I were very unsure of each other. We were more like strangers to each other than when we were first married! We felt very insecure. There were no established boundaries upon our relationship. Each disagreement seemed to blow up all out of proportion. We were both confused. I felt like I was not good enough for her. It seemed the task of winning her confidence and love back was going to be too hard for me.
>
> Not knowing any other way to cope, our first attempts to deal with the stress of the fragile situation

was to merely occupy the same house while allowing no need or trust to exist between us. This, of course, solved nothing. Trying to live together while ignoring each other was a foolish form of retreat which destroyed rather than built our relationship. ...With such an impenetrable defensive shield between us, and without tolerance and understanding, neither of us was able to give or receive the love which our marriage needed. (p. 55, 73)

This is a crucial time in a relationship. At this point, many will decide to give up and quit. Those who do feel impressed by the Lord to try to overcome the effects of infidelity must be aware that the adversary will fight every effort to heal. Satan does not want them to succeed in healing and forgiving "for he persuadeth no man to do good, no, not one; neither do his angels; neither do they who subject themselves unto him." (Moroni 7:17)

Many couples go through an intense several months after a spouse's confession of infidelity, or after infidelity has been discovered in a partner, which becomes a testing, trying time that will determine whether the relationship will outlast this critical, crucial period. Satan will put all of his negative forces to work at this time in order to destroy that eternal relationship. He knows the destructive rippling effects that destroying an eternal family has.

Satan already has a foothold in one of the spouse's lives, a foothold he will not let go of easily as he continues to cultivate a straying spouse's anger for a partner and as he continues to help form rationalizations and justifications for sins committed. But it must be taken into account that the adversary also aims his works of destruction at those who have remained faithful. Those betrayed spouses often feel insecure, unsettled and uncertain of the path they should choose for them and their families. During this time of vulnerability, Satan many times plants seeds of doubt that the relationship will ever heal or he may play upon the feelings of distrust and hurt of the one betrayed. He wants these people to leave—to give up, to go on and to move forward without trying to heal their marriage—for then he can continue on with the destruction he's effectively begun.

Satan whispered to one woman who was dealing with her husband's transgressions, "The Lord knows your marriage is going to fail. He is preparing you for it to fail. Work toward being on your own." She felt accompanying confusion and distress with these whisperings and felt troubled and anxious as these thoughts bombarded her constantly. It wasn't until the Lord warned her through a priesthood blessing that the fruits of His impressions were peace and calm and that the fruits of Satan's whisperings were confusion that she could discern that the thoughts given to her had come from the adversary. She decidedly put her whole heart and efforts into healing her marriage. Her relationship was able to move toward healing and she felt thankful that the words of God "divide[d] asunder all the cunning and the snares and the wiles of the devil." (Helaman 3:29)

"If Ye Will Have Faith in Me Ye Shall Have Power to Do Whatsoever Thing is Expedient in Me" (Moroni 7:33)

Many have spoken of special gifts of strength and sustenance given to them from the Savior during the crucial time when a sinning spouse is making the decision whether or not to return to the relationship or whether or not to leave that relationship. These seem to be the compensatory blessings He has promised those who try to follow Him, blessings which will come as those who have been betrayed work to overcome what has happened to them. As Richard G. Scott has said:

> I testify that when the Lord closes one important door in your life, he shows his continuing love and compassion by opening many other compensating doors through your exercise of faith. He will place in your path packets of spiritual sunlight to brighten your way. They often come after the trial has been the greatest, as evidence of the compassion and love of an all-knowing Father. (*Ensign*, Nov. 1995)

These gifts and blessings many times come about in unique, personalized ways. For example, Allison felt she was given a special gift of outward beauty during the time her husband was deciding whether or not to leave her. This unsurpassed beauty she was given lasted for a period of several weeks. Her husband said to her some time later as their marriage relationship began to heal, "Even when we were at the worst of our problems, I still always thought you were beautiful." Allison felt she was given this gift of beauty because the Lord wanted to help her husband make his choices without taking away his free agency. She also felt the gift had been given to help her with her own self-confidence and self-esteem as she dealt with feelings of hurt and rejection. "I could look at myself and still feel proud of who I was," she said. She knew this was a blessing from the Lord to help her combat the injustices that had come upon her.

One woman was told through a special priesthood blessing that people who would come to help, serve and strengthen her during times of difficulty were a blessing from Him and to accept their physical and emotional support as evidence of the Lord's love and compassion for her. Others have been blessed with righteous priesthood holders or other righteous counselors willing to help them deal with their hardships by listening, directing, sustaining and counseling them through their trials.

One woman was admonished by the Lord through a priesthood blessing to seek the help of priesthood leaders to overcome the problems in her marriage. The Lord told her He would justify her in seeking this outside help and reinforcement because it was a need that she had to remain whole, secure and emotionally healthy. She was also directed to ask for a priesthood blessing whenever she felt she needed it. The Lord promised her through the blessings that He would continue to give her direction and the counsel she needed each step of the way to deal with whatever would befall her in the future.

The Lord will give blessings such as this to any who are willing to follow Him. Many who have followed the prompting of the Lord to stay within broken marriages find that, despite hardships they may face or have faced, that they become "stronger and stronger in their humility, and firmer and firmer in the faith of Christ, unto the filling their souls with joy and consolation, yea, even to the purifying and the sanctification of their hearts, which sanctification cometh because of their yielding their hearts unto God." (Helaman 3:35) Many find peace amidst times of further trial and can continue to serve others despite difficulties they may be experiencing. Others find joy and happiness in happenings outside their marriages despite trials within them. This is because these people know they are following the will of the Savior and have been given compensatory blessings to sustain them through their hardships.

Dealing With the Contentious Behavior of a Spouse

One of the greatest hardships in dealing with spouses who have strayed is that "Satan has great hold upon their hearts; he stirreth them up to iniquity against that which is good." (D&C

10:20) Often, too, those "in whom you have trusted [have] sought to destroy you" (D&C 10:6) and will continue to try to hurt and destroy. It is a horrendous burden to have to work with straying spouses who will anger easily, attack, belittle, undermine and try to harm those with whom they have made covenants. It is difficult to move forward in such a relationship where trust has been destroyed and where straying parties continue to turn against that which is good. For example, when one wife would mention to her excommunicated husband that she had attended the temple during the day, he would turn on her angrily and say that she was "self-righteous" and that she was "throwing it all in his face to try to hurt him" because he couldn't go himself. It got to the point that she would not share with him the knowledge that she'd gone to the temple because of his contentious reactions.

Even if the Lord calls upon one to deal with this type of contention, this person does not have to become subjected to the verbal abuses, attacks or injustices that will come. The Lord through a priesthood blessing told one woman who was dealing with difficulties in her marriage relationship that her first priority in her relationship was to strengthen and protect herself. She felt the Lord direct her to leave any situation in which her husband became angry and vengeful toward her as they discussed problems they had. She felt the Lord prompt her to take much-needed individual time in which she could heal from contentious behavior she'd experienced when she did interact with her husband.

Those dealing with contention should remember that the Lord does not require them to deal with contention and difficulty at their own eternal expense. They should *never* blindly live with any type of physical, verbal, emotional or other types of abuse. Lisa told of the experience she had after her husband had been unfaithful to her. Despite the pain her husband had caused, Lisa wanted to stay with her husband and protect her marriage at all costs. She wanted her children to have a father and she wanted the financial security of staying with her husband, even at the sacrifice of a healthy marriage relationship and her own pain.

Lisa continued to be the object of derision and anger from her husband as she stayed with him. When the contention between them grew and increased to an ever greater extent to the point where Lisa could no longer withstand it, she turned in desperation to the Lord. She in essence told the Lord that although she had wanted to stay with her husband, she would now open up her heart to do whatever the Lord required of her—even if it meant leaving her husband and trying to provide for her young family on her own. Lisa would now relinquish her will to His and do whatever He asked, even if it meant forging a life for her and her children by herself.

Lisa said that it seemed as if the Lord had been waiting for her to relinquish her will to His the entire time she had been dealing with her relationship. She felt a sense of peace and comfort as the Lord accepted her offering to follow Him. He whispered through an impression into her mind, "It is enough." Lisa came to understand through further impressions that her offering to follow the Lord's will at whatever the cost—even if it meant divorce and hardship—had been similar to Abraham's offering of obedience to offer up his son, Isaac. She now knew her offering of obedience had been sufficient.

Lisa soon after told her husband of her willingness and determination to leave their marriage if his behaviors didn't change. Although there were subsequently two times of crisis where they began to make the move toward separation and divorce, ultimately they were able to save their marriage. Today their marriage has become strong and healthy. Lisa felt like it was a blessing from the Lord because of her promised obedience to Him, that "inasmuch as [she was] humble, [she] might be made strong" (D&C 1:28) and "reap eternal joy for all [her] sufferings." (D&C 109:76) She knew also that the Lord had not expected her to suffer needlessly for her husband's transgressions but had prepared a way for her escape. This is true for any who are victims of infidelity. As the Lord said to Joseph Smith, "Behold, I have seen your sacrifices, and will forgive all your sins; I have seen your sacrifices in obedience to that which I have told you. Go, therefore, and I make a way for your escape, as I accepted the offering of Abraham of his son Isaac." (D&C 132:50)

"The Lord God Will Help Me, Therefore I Shall Not Be Confounded" (2 Nephi 7:7)

Those who have accepted the will of the Lord to stay with their sinning spouses and feel prompted to help them repent must remember that "all victory and glory is brought to pass unto you through your diligence, faithfulness, and prayers of faith." (D&C 103:36) Many times these people will be given inspired words to help them through "for it shall be given you in the very hour, yea, in the very moment, what ye shall say." (D&C 100:6) One woman was told in a blessing that she should not be afraid to chastise her husband, that he would know she was speaking the will of the Lord through the Holy Ghost. "A commandment I give unto you, that ye shall declare whatsoever thing ye declare in my name, in solemnity of heart, in the spirit of meekness, in all things. And I give unto you this promise, that inasmuch as ye do this the Holy Ghost shall be shed forth in bearing record unto all things whatsoever ye shall say." (D&C 100:7-8)

Straying parties' reaction to chastisement may be similar

to Laman's and Lemuel's reactions to Nephi's chastisement: "Ye have murmured because he hath been plain unto you," their father, Lehi, described their reactions. "Ye say that he hath used sharpness; ye say that he hath been angry with you; but behold, his sharpness was the sharpness of the power of the word of God, which was in him; and that which ye call anger was the truth, according to that which is in God, which he could not restrain, manifesting boldly concerning your iniquities." (2 Nephi 1:26) Though these types of responses may happen, those calling sinning spouses to repentance may move forward in faith knowing that "the weakness of their words will I make strong in their faith." (2 Nephi 3:21) As the scriptures state:

> The Lord will help me, therefore I will not be confounded.
> ...The Lord is near, and he justifieth me. Who will contend with me? Let us stand together. Who is mine adversary? Let him come near me, and I will smite him with the strength of my mouth.
> For the Lord God will help me. (2 Nephi 7:7-9)

Finding Forgiveness

Elder Richard G. Scott has reminded us that we must "honestly forgive as often as is required. The Lord declared: 'If he...repenteth in the sincerity of his heart, him shall ye forgive, and I will forgive him also. ...And as often as my people repent will I forgive them' [Mosiah 26:29-30]." (*Ensign*, May 1988) For many, forgiving is an extremely difficult step, especially if a spouse has not yet become repentant. The injustices that will come will make those who have been hurt want to harbor anger and bitterness. The Lord knows this. He knows the difficult emotions those wounded must deal with when they are betrayed. He knows the difficulty of forgiving injustices that still continue to come, sometimes daily or hourly.

The Lord was wrongly and unjustly blamed. He was hated and resented when his offerings of love and service were always perfect. He knows what it is like to be unfairly accused and misunderstood. He understands perfectly the emotions and hardship of what happens. Forgiveness, then, will only come as a gift from the Savior and our Father in Heaven—who know that only through forgiveness can we find personal healing and peace. They will help individuals define what forgiveness means in each circumstance and then they will help carry the burden of forgiving.

"They continue to love us perfectly," Richard G. Scott has said, "each one of us, individually. Yes, they are all-powerful and all-knowing; their works extend eternally, yet their love for each of us is personal, knowing, uncompromising, endless, perfect." (*Ensign*, May 1998) Because of this love, they will extend the mercy, love and patience needed toward the one trying to forgive a sinning spouse as much as they will extend help to a transgressor. Feelings of love, patience, forgiveness and mercy will come from them as very real gifts.

Janelle would approach the Lord with each new injustice her husband thrust upon her because of his transgressions. As each new injustice came, the Lord would bless her with the forgiveness necessary for each specific incident. Sometimes forgiveness would take weeks, but other times she felt forgiveness come immediately and instantaneously. These blessings were specific feelings that would give her the necessary understanding, compassion, patience and the ability to forget wrongs done or to let those wrongs go to the Savior, who she knew would handle them justly.

During this process, Janelle would often feel the Savior forgive her own indiscretions, weaknesses and sins, sometimes without her even asking. As He showed her in her own personal life how this forgiveness would come as a free, very real gift from Him with peace, comfort and love to accompany it, she became better able to forgive her husband for the deep and continuing wrongs he did to her.

During forgiveness of her sins, Janelle felt no reproach, anger or resentment from the Lord. She *felt* Him forgive her. The Savior taught her from His own forgiveness how to begin to forgive her husband. When she sometimes felt despair come due to her inability to forgive the hurt that still came from her husband's contentious behavior, she felt the Savior protect and strengthen her until she could move forward again, independent of her husband or what he thought of her efforts. Janelle also discovered that the Lord was as patient with her inability to forgive as He was with her husband's inability to repent completely and immediately of his wrongdoing. Janelle knew it would be an ongoing process and that as long as she was willing and prayerful, the Lord would help her through it.

The Lord has said, "If ye will come unto me ye shall have eternal life. Behold, mine arm of mercy is extended towards you, and whosoever will come, him will I receive; and blessed are those who come unto me." (3 Nephi 9:14) Elder Marvin J. Ashton said, "This scripture indicates that in life there is no waiting period before we can come unto God. In our weakness we know where we can turn for strength. ...As one comes unto Christ, he learns of the reality of forgiveness: 'Behold, he who has repented of his sins, the same is forgiven, and I, the Lord, remember them no more.' (D&C 58:42)" (*Ensign*, May 1988)

8

"Whosoever Repenteth and Cometh Unto Me, the Same is My Church" (D&C 10:67)

As mentioned previously, a spouse who has been betrayed will often be the one instrumental in helping a straying spouse move toward repentance. If those straying spouses "reject not my words, which shall be established by the testimony which shall be given, blessed are they, and then shall ye have joy in the fruit of your labors." (D&C 6:31) One must never forget, however, that the choice for repentance must ultimately come from the one who has transgressed. "Ye shall deny yourselves of all ungodliness," the scriptures tell us, "and love God with all your might, mind and strength, *then is his grace sufficient for you."* (Moroni 10:32, italics added) Healing can come in a marriage *only if* those who have transgressed strive for cleansing from their sins and *only if* they move from the darkness they have chosen back toward the light.

"There is one crucial test of repentance," President Spencer W. Kimball has told us. "This is abandonment of sin." (*Miracle of Forgiveness*, p. 163) He further states:

> In abandoning sin...one should avoid the places and conditions and circumstances where the sin occurred, for these could most readily breed it again. He must abandon the people with whom the sin was committed. He may not hate the persons involved but he must avoid them and everything associated with the sin. He must dispose of all letters,

trinkets, and things which will remind him of the "old days" and the "old times." He must forget addresses, telephone numbers, people, places and situations from the sinful past, and build a new life. He must eliminate anything which would stir the old memories. *(The Miracle of Forgiveness, p. 171)*

Confession to the proper ecclesiastical authorities is also an essential element of proper repentance, for "by this ye may know if a man repenteth of his sins—behold, he will confess them and forsake them." (D&C 58:43) Unless a straying party is willing to confess and counsel with the proper priesthood authorities, the possibility of healing a damaged relationship becomes virtually nonexistent.

One man described the change of heart he had after his confession. Before this time, he had toyed with not confessing, feeling that he could justify his sexual sins to the point where they would not require this step. He described his feelings after subsequently following his wife's urgings to go see their bishop and confess fully: "It was almost as if [from this step] that the Lord touched my heart and changed it. I felt clean. I no longer wanted to sin. I no longer had the slightest desire to sin." Although this man did not cease to struggle with his shortcomings and pitfalls after this time—or the resulting difficulties within his marriage, he felt the Lord's strength come to him often as he tried to make necessary deep-rooted changes. The Lord has said,

> Behold, ye are little children and ye cannot bear all things now; ye must grow in grace and in the knowledge of truth.
> Fear not, little children, for you are mine, and I have overcome the world, and you are of them that my Father hath given me;
> And none of them that my Father hath given me shall be lost. (D&C 50:40-42)

Elder Richard G. Scott once stated:

> The overcoming of serious transgression follows a pattern. First and foremost, it is the internal battle, the crosscurrent of feeling, the anguish about being found out, the worry about the impact on other lives, and the fear of the unknown. This struggle is prolonged through indecision, and that means more pain and further damage. It can be cut short through decisive personal commitment to clean up your life now. Right now. Once that decision is made, there follow many individual decisions and acts, none of which is overpowering. Yet taken together, they will kill the monster controlling your life.
>
> The most difficult part about changing is to make an unwavering decision to do it, and when required, to enlist the help of your bishop. Once that beginning is made, you will find the rest of the path becomes easier than you imagined. Some days are more difficult than others, but the process becomes easier because through your use of agency, you qualify for the Lord's help, and He magnifies your efforts. [See Omni 1:26]. (*Ensign*, May 1990)

Spencer W. Kimball further reminded those who have transgressed, "To every forgiveness there is a condition. The plaster must be as wide as the sore. The fasting, the prayers, the humility must be equal to or greater than the sin." (*The Miracle of Forgiveness*, p. 353) It is only when straying parties choose to take these steps that healing will occur. Healing in relationships will come only after those who have transgressed turn their lives over to the Savior. Then, as the Savior did for the followers of Alma the Elder:

> He changed their hearts; yea, he awakened them out of a deep sleep, and they awoke unto God. Behold, they were in the midst of darkness;

187

nevertheless, their souls were illuminated by the light of the everlasting word; yea, they were encircled about by the bands of death, and the chains of hell, and an everlasting destruction did await them.

And now I ask of you, my brethren, were they destroyed? Behold, I say unto you, Nay, they were not.

And again I ask, were the bands of death broken, and the chains of hell which encircled them about, were they loosed? I say unto you, Yea, they were loosed, and their souls did expand, and they did sing redeeming love. And I say unto you that they are saved. (Alma 5:7-9)

"Leave Judgment Alone with Me, For it is Mine and I Will Repay" (D&C 82:23)

Elder Scott has warned those who have been damaged by the transgressions of others:

> When anguish comes from evil acts of others, there should be punishment and corrective action taken, but the offended is not the one to initiate that action. Leave it to others who have that responsibility. Learn to forgive; though terribly hard, it will release you and open the way to a newness of life. Time devoted by one injured to ensure the offender is punished is time wasted in the healing process. (*Ensign*, May 1994)

The Lord has told us that, "Vengeance is mine, and I will repay." (Mormon 3:15) Victims who carry the burdens of another's sins need to remember that the Lord will be the one to execute judgment on those who have harmed them. It is not their responsibility to do so. They need to remember, as well, that despite the close proximity they might live to transgressors, they will not be able to judge transgressors' hearts on their own. It is only the Lord who intimately knows the thoughts and intents of the heart. (D&C 6:16)

Annette was reminded of this as she dealt with the transgressions of her husband. She would often feel a compulsive need to question and re-question him about his intents—about his desires to change, about his desires to heal their marriage and about his desires to become clean and "bring forth fruit meet for repentance." (Alma 12:15) Annette found that despite her husband's positive assurances that he was trying to do these things, she could not believe him or trust him, especially knowing he'd broken his promises to her previously by his transgressions.

Annette became continually troubled over their relationship, unable to move forward in it. As she recorded in writing at this time, "I've been struggling with many ups and downs, turning to Christ once again for the only healing power I know or have. Struggles continue with [my husband]. I long for the love, admiration and respect I had for him. I feel a great loss trying to come to terms with all this. Sometimes I feel complete and whole (with the Lord's help) and I can love him unconditionally, but sometimes I feel a great void in our marriage, a searing loneliness that leaves me in tears. I cannot share much of my misery with [my husband], a blessing I have taken for granted before. I'm turning to the Lord for further, much-needed help."

As Annette continued to struggle like this, the Lord whispered into her mind one day that it would be impossible to know her husband's heart on her own, that only the Lord knew it and when necessary, He could reveal it and make it known unto her. She came to understand from this divine revelation that the Lord could direct her and lead her in accordance to what He knew of her husband's heart and desires, not according to what she supposed she saw in their relationship. She came to understand that her own thoughts, views, experiences and judgments were inadequate and she could not rely on them.

As Annette turned to the Savior for this type of guidance, the Lord often impressed upon her mind, through the scriptures and through priesthood blessings, where her husband was at in his progress. The turning point came in their relationship when the Lord revealed to Annette that her husband was willing and trying desperately hard to hearken to Him, to hear His voice and follow His counsel.

With this reassurance—without seeing fully the fruits of this change in her husband's life or the fruits of repentance in their relationship, but only going forward in faith—Annette could better open up her heart to her husband and work with him, knowing with a certainty that he was trying to change and do the Lord's will. Subsequently, little by little, "line upon line, precept upon precept, here a little and there a little," (2 Nephi 28:30) her husband began to make the changes required of him to become whole. As these changes happened, the positive changes in their marriage were a natural result. As the scriptures state:

> Put your trust in that Spirit which leadeth to do good—yea, to do justly, to walk humbly, to judge righteously; and this is my Spirit.
>
> Verily, verily, I say unto you, I will impart unto you of my Spirit, which shall enlighten your mind, which shall fill your soul with joy;
>
> And then shall ye know, or by this shall you know, all things whatsoever you desire of me, which are pertaining unto things of righteousness, in faith believing in me that you shall receive. (D&C 11:12-14)

9

"Unto That Soul Who Sinneth Shall the Former Sins Return" (D&C 82:7)

The Lord has said, "I, the Lord, will not lay any sin to your charge; go your ways and sin no more; but unto that soul who sinneth shall the former sins return." (D&C 82:7) Transgressors who have broken sacred eternal covenants need to remember this important element in their repentance process—that there needs be a complete forsaking of sin before any lasting healing in their lives or relationships will occur. Elder Malcolm S. Jeppsen of the Seventy once said:

> All too often I have seen those who have repented slip some time later into their old sinful ways. When that happens, previously repented sins return to those who perhaps did not really repent after all.
>
> ...There must be a compliance with all the commandments of God. This means that those guilty of serious transgressions who are repentant haven't fully repented until they become full tithe payers, or fully overcome Word of Wisdom problems, are morally clean, or keep the Sabbath day holy. (*Ensign*, May 1994)

Elder Marvin J. Ashton once gave a prescription for transgressors that can be used to help them not fall back into sinful patterns. He said:

SHUN FEELINGS OF RESENTMENT, BITTERNESS AND CONTENTION TOWARD INDIVI-

DUALS RENDERING DECISIONS. When discipline is administered, there is a tendency on the part of some to become resentful toward the individuals and institutions who have had to make the judgment. ...Resentment and anger are not good for the soul. They are foul things.

Bitterness must be replaced with humility.

...A repentant individual will choose his own course and proceed with confidence. He has no need to protect a wounded self. He will not allow himself the danger of self-inflicted sympathy. It is generally good medicine to sympathize with others, but not with yourself.

The second step he recommends is to:

SHUN DISCOURAGEMENT. One of Satan's most powerful tools is discouragement. Whisperings of "you can't do it," "you're no good," "it's too late," "what's the use?" or "things are hopeless" are tools of destruction. Satan...wants you to quit trying. It is important that discouragement is cast out of the lives of those who are waiting.

The third step he suggests is to:

SHUN ESCAPE ROUTES. ...It is easier to demean and place blame on others for our situation than it is to repent and grow.

One man recalls a time in his repentance process that he turned in prayer to the Lord, complaining to the Lord about all the negative behaviors his wife had, all the mistakes she'd made in their marriage and all the hurts she'd caused him, claiming she was "selfish." The Lord whispered into his mind as this man spoke to Him, "You are the one being selfish."

Though this statement was hard for him to accept, it deeply humbled and chastened him. From that point forward, this man could begin to make the necessary changes in his own life without blaming his wife for his problems. He made changes which made it possible for him to move toward proper repentance and the ultimate healing of his marriage.

Elder Ashton continues:

> SHUN THE DESIRE TO BECOME ANONY-MOUS. When difficulties arise, some want to fade into the crowd and become lost and unknown. ...There is a wonderful support system available to those who are listed on the records of the Church. There are those who will listen, help and teach. There will be opportunities to study scriptures, ponder, and pray. Caring people and a caring God want to know where you are.
>
> All need to be known, recognized, and loved. Hearts and souls reach out for nurturing and meaningful association. Even those who claim they want to be left alone are in reality seeking their own identity.
>
> ...PARTICIPATE IN "REPORTING IN." Part of your responsibility in coming back is to find someone with whom you can share your concerns, questions and progress.
>
> ...Look for this kind of person in your life. Problems often seem to diminish when they are vocalized. ...It is comforting to have a listener who will share your feelings and respect your needs.

Most importantly, he reminds us:

> Everyone can "report in" to an under-standing Father who loves all His children. God knows the feelings in every human heart. He can soften sorrow and lead when there seems to be no light. Prayer can give guidance and confidence. ...No one need be alone in this world. If all else fails, remember: God and one other person can be a family.
> (*Ensign*, May 1988)

"Light and Truth Forsake That Evil One" (D&C 99:28)

The only way someone can ultimately overcome sin is by accepting light and truth and continuing on in the paths of truth. Richard G. Scott once reminded us:

> No one can change truth. Rationalization, overpowering self-interest, all of the arguments of men, anger or self-will cannot change truth.
> Obedience to [the Savior's commandments]...is the only way to permanently cure the damage to mind and spirit caused by unrighteous acts.

He then spoke to those trying to change their sinful lives. He stated:

> You may have found that change is hard. But know you can do it. You may wonder why you are not believed when you decide to change from a life of disobedience to one of integrity and compliance to truth. Recognize that it takes time to build a reputation that overcomes the effects of past deliberate decisions to deceive and to take advantage of others—but it is worth it.
> Where there is purity of heart and real intent, it is known to the Lord. Your obedience to truth and proper use of agency open the door to His divine help. At first, perhaps only you and He will believe your sincerity. But you will be rewarded by the joy that comes from positive personal progress. In time, others will recognize your consistent righteous acts and support you.
> I testify that the Savior heals permanently. ...I testify that the Savior will heal you as you choose to obey truth and use your agency according to His counsel. (*Ensign*, Nov. 1992)

One man bore his testimony of the Savior's healing power from his own personal experience. He had once experienced a period of time in his life where he had been deeply involved in darkness, sin and deception. When he heard of a close friend going through the difficulties of similar transgressions, he said, "All I could think of is how awful it must be for my friend. You feel so mixed up and confused when you are sinning. You feel like you're leading a double life. You can barely stand the darkness and the deceit you know you're involved in. I hated it. I hated the feelings I had then. I'll never forget the day when the Lord touched my heart and changed me. It made me literally free. I no longer had the desire to sin. I never want to feel as badly as I did then."

The Savior once said:

> Have ye any that are sick among you...or that are afflicted in any manner? Bring them hither and I will heal them, for I have compassion upon you; my bowels are filled with mercy.
> ...*I see that your faith is sufficient that I should heal you.*
> And it came to pass that when he had thus spoken, all the multitude, with one accord, did go forth...and *he did heal them* every one as they were brought forth unto him.
> And they did all, both they who had been healed and they who were whole, bow down at his feet, and did worship him. (3 Nephi 17:7-10, italics added)

The Savior truly can heal those who have transgressed if they will return to Him. "Return ye now every one from his evil way," the Lord has said, "and make your ways and your doings good." (Jeremiah 18:11) Then He promises, "I will forgive their iniquity, and I will remember their sin no more." (Jeremiah 31:34)

"They Went About Zealously Striving to Repair All the Injuries Which They Had Done" (Mosiah 27:35)

Another element of proper repentance is repairing as

much as one can the damage done by infidelity. For one man, he made effort upon effort to do small acts of service and incessant shows of love toward his wife as he repented. "I wanted to try to make up for all the things I put her through," he said. Because of this, there came to be a resurgence of love and caring back into their relationship.

Another man who had transgressed once said, "Here I went about looking for all the things I supposed I wanted in a woman. I had no idea all the things I wanted existed in the one standing right in front of me." His words gave deep comfort and assurance to his wife, who had remained faithful to him during his times of transgression. Through such words and other efforts, he tried to show his wife the changes wrought in him.

Steven A. Cramer said:

> A major part of [my] repentance required that I establish proper relationships with my wife and children. My emotions and affections had to be transformed from the former feelings of resentment and indifference to feelings of appreciation and genuine love and interest.
>
> [Healing] is not so simple as merely refraining from the specific transgression. It is, rather, a process of correcting many other faults which have formed barriers between the person and the Lord. I am talking about faults such as my improper feelings toward my family. I am talking about the exchange of hate, envy, grudges, bitterness and malice for the sweet peace of forgiveness, tolerance, respect and love. I am talking about the exchange of selfishness and preoccupation with self for an interest in the happiness and well-being of others. (*The Worth of a Soul*, p. 75)

A Mighty Change of Heart

King Benjamin's people spoke of a time that the "Spirit

of the Lord Omnipotent...has wrought a mighty change in us, or in our hearts, that we have no more disposition to do evil, but to do good continually." (Mosiah 5:2) This "mighty change" may come about for anyone willing to submit a heart, mind, desires and personal will to the Lord.

Corihor, a little-known Jaredite who was the son of Kib, "repented of the many evils which he had done" after a lifetime of wickedness. (Ether 7:13) The Lord truly must have, as he did for King Benjamin's people, blessed Corihor with this "mighty change" of heart. The Lord can heal and make anyone who has transgressed become whole again, even after a lifetime of sin and wickedness. Steven A. Cramer put it this way:

> All my life I had been tormented by the struggle between the carnal part of me that craved pornography and self-love and the spiritual part of me that wanted to love and obey God. Now at last I could see that through those thirty years I had been struggling to control my behavior, I was only working on the symptom. The real problem was not my behavior, but my *human nature, which only the Lord could change.* (The Worth of a Soul, p. 91, italics added)

The Lord can indeed change hearts, wills and desires—our very natures—if we will only but "offer up [our] whole souls as an offering unto him." (Omni 1:26) As Neal A. Maxwell once said, "Becoming more like Jesus in thought and behavior is not grinding and repressing, but emancipating and discovering!" (*Ensign*, Nov. 1992) The Lord has promised, "And ye shall know the truth, and the truth shall make you *free.*" (John 8:32, italics added) The scriptures tell us:

> Yea, I say unto you come and fear not, and lay aside every sin, which easily doth beset you, which doth bind you down to destruction, yea, come

and go forth, and show unto your God that ye are willing to repent of your sins and enter into a covenant with him to keep his commandments. And whosoever doeth this, and keepeth the commandments of God from thenceforth, the same will remember that I say unto him, yea, he will remember that I have said unto him, he shall have eternal life, according to the testimony of the Holy Spirit, which testifieth in me. (Alma 7: 15-16)

10

Healing and Forgiveness

In *The Worth of A Soul*, author Steven A. Cramer stated:

> A great puzzle of my excommunication experience was my wife's complete and total forgiveness. I fully expected her to expel me from the home and family. I was almost positive that she would seek a divorce. Yet she forgave, willingly and freely. It was so Christ-like. How could she do that from the very depths of her sorrow?
>
> Another puzzle was how she could endure the insufferable way that I treated the family during those two horrible years when my emotions were under Satanic influence. No one in their right mind would endure what she endured. I totally deserved to be rejected. No one could have criticized or condemned her for insisting that I leave the home when my presence was so evil and depressing. Yet she bore the multitude of injustices I imposed upon her and the children patiently and kindly, almost passively. Her response to me was like the silent, submissive attitude of the Savior.
>
> How could my wife endure her suffering without protesting and fighting back? How could she continue to believe in me when I was so despicable and when there was not even the slightest clue that I would ever improve?
>
> The answers to these questions are of great importance to all who are facing the stress of a similar situation. The truth of the matter is that, on her own, my wife was not able to react in this

manner. She couldn't have. No one could! The truth is that *she was blessed and endowed through the grace of God with the ability to treat me as He, Himself, would treat me. Because her desire to be in harmony with the Lord's will was paramount in her heart, the Lord actually loaned her the ability to feel and act as He would want her to act!* (p. 72, italics added)

Many who have overcome problems relating to infidelity can testify of the truth of this statement, that the Lord will bless, sustain and endow those who are trying to overcome in faith the consequences of a spouse's unfaithfulness. Once they are willing to align their wills with the Savior's desires for them, He will strengthen and carry them through whatever will befall them. The Lord will also bless those who turn to Him with the necessary forgiveness—sometimes daily forgiveness—for the unrighteous actions of their spouses. He will be there to lift, comfort, buoy and "speak peace to [their] souls" as they turn to Him. (Alma 58:11) He will always be waiting, willing and able to bring lasting healing and wholeness to relationships scarred by infidelity.

Light at the End of the Tunnel

One woman spoke of the experiences she had that testified of the Savior's sustenance and help. She said, "When my husband first came to me and made his confessions [of unfaithfulness], for a tiny moment the Lord opened up my mind and let me glimpse into the future. In that one second, the Lord let me see that there would come a time in our relationship where there would be complete healing, where it would be seem as if my husband's indiscretions had never happened.

"This feeling of wholeness became a lifeline to me as I struggled over the next long months and years dealing with my husband's transgressions. I often wondered if this prompting had been correct or if it had only been wishful thinking on my part. Sometimes the hardships were too great to bear and I felt separation and possibly divorce would be the only option.

"The Savior literally carried me through these hard times. There were times when I actually felt His presence near me—loving, sustaining, pulling me along with outstretched arms. The Savior spoke to me constantly through the scriptures and through priesthood blessings. He filled me with peace and wholeness often when I attended the temple. He gave me a sister who understood what I was experiencing and who helped me by listening and caring. He gave me friends who brought meals and who did other acts of kindness when I was at my lowest times.

"The Savior's promise to me is being fulfilled. My marriage has become better. The Savior was able to take the pain and heartache of it and help me with it, putting us where we are today."

Another woman spoke of the hard experiences she'd gone through at one period in her life after her husband's betrayal before his divorcing her. She knew the path she would have to travel would be long and that the way would be dark, difficult and hard, but whenever she saw this darkness in her mind—and the long, dark tunnel she would have to travel—she would always envision "the light at the end of the tunnel." It was as if the Savior was letting her get a glimpse of the eternal promises that awaited her as she struggled in faith to do what He required of her. Healing such as this comes from a life centered on the Savior.

One woman said of her incredible hardships, "It's like weightlifting. When you lift weights, you destroy a layer of muscle. But what you build on that layer is stronger than what it ever was before. I'm so glad I went through what I did or I wouldn't be as strong as I am today."

Another woman said that in overcoming the problems of her husband's unfaithfulness, she and her husband had to go back to the early stages of their marriage and deal with every problem they had ever faced during the whole of their relationship, even those once-buried and forgotten. As they overcame these problems one by one, "What we have today is far better than what it ever was, even before [my husband's transgressions]. I would never go back to what we had before. This is so much better."

Another woman said, "I remember hearing about a thirty-day survival camp from a friend. All the people there would say afterward, 'I'll never go through that again but I would never give up the experiences I had going through it.' I feel the same way about the hardships we experienced in our marriage. I would never go through them again but I'm glad that I did go through them. My faith and trust in the Savior is stronger than it's ever been. I don't know if I'd be at this point without having gone through what I did."

Steven A. Cramer's wife wrote that after their experiences, her husband was...

> ...undeniably a changed man. This change was reflected in every aspect of his life, but I noticed it in our marriage relationship and in his relationships with our children. It was such an amazing change that it took me several months to comprehend that it was real and honest. Now I truly understand that when the Lord affects a healing, He heals the whole man from the inside out.
>
> I am experiencing for the first time the love of a man rich in kindness, tolerance and compassion; a man who truly loves the Lord and can feel and express gratitude. He has become a man who lets wisdom rule his interaction with his children and not

temper or intolerance. He has become, at last, the head of our family and has in every way justified our faith in him and earned our respect and love. (*The Worth of a Soul*, p. 107)

"Now, my brethren, we see that God is mindful of every people, whatsoever land they may be in; yea, he numbereth his people, and his bowels of mercy are over all the earth," Ammon has reminded us. (Alma 26:37) Truly the Savior's mercy becomes evident in the healing of any relationship once scarred by infidelity.

"Bear With Patience Thine Afflictions, and I Will Give Unto You Success" (Alma 26:27)

Many couples dealing with the repercussions of infidelity have come to be able to talk openly with understanding and kindness about the experiences they've gone through and the hurts they've suffered in the past. Although many have taken years of effort and trial to reach this point, those who do so express their deep and lasting gratitude for the Savior who has been able to effect such changes in their lives and in their marriages.

Many transgressors have come forward in humility and sorrow, asking a spouse's forgiveness for all they have put their spouses and families through by their unrighteous behaviors. Many couples have been able to resolve the difficulties, pains and contentious issues of the past and now "hav[e] their hearts knit together in unity and in love one towards another." (Mosiah 18:21) Though this truly can be an undertaking that might encompass years, the Lord has said, "Let your hearts be comforted; for *all things* shall work together for good to them that walk uprightly, and to the sanctification of the church." (D&C 100:15, italics added)

The Lord has given promise upon promise that He will

always be there for us during our difficulties and trials, that He will never forsake us and that He will guide, comfort, love us and fill us with His peace during times of hardship. He has given assurance upon assurance that He knows our weaknesses and how to "succor" us. (D&C 62:1) The Lord has repeatedly reminded us that "he who is faithful shall overcome *all things*." (D&C 75:16, italics added) "Such may receive a more exceeding and eternal weight of glory," He has said. (D&C 63:66) Therefore He tells us, "Continue your journey and let your hearts rejoice; for behold, and lo, *I am with you even unto the end*." (D&C 100:12, italics added) The Lord has said:

> Ye cannot behold with your natural eyes, for the present time, the design of your God concerning those things which shall come hereafter, and the glory which shall follow after much tribulation.
>
> For after much tribulation come the blessings. Wherefore the day cometh that ye shall be crowned with much glory; the hour is not yet, but is nigh at hand.
>
> ...Remember this, which I tell you before, that you may lay it to heart, and receive that which is to follow. (D&C 58:3-5)